My Generation

by the same author

British Trade Unions and
The Problem of Change

My Generation

Will Paynter

London . George Allen & Unwin Ltd
Ruskin House   Museum Street

ISBN 0 04 923057 3 cased
     0 04 923058 1 paper

Printed in Great Britain
in 11 point Baskerville type
by Clarke, Doble & Brendon Ltd
Plymouth

Contents

Chapter 1

Introduction

Some of my younger friends and colleagues suggested that I should write an autobiography. Initially, I had some misgivings about doing this, because such projects can so easily descend to being no more than a chronicle of personal exploits, much embellished in the telling and finally appearing as an exercise in self-glorification. My friends, however, were obviously not interested in that kind of subjective story but rather in the events covered by the period of my active life and in which I played some small part. Their interest was more in a history of my generation as witnessed and portrayed through my eyes and experiences.

Much is written and said these days about the so-called generation gap as if it were some new social phenomenon. At the end of the sixteenth century, Shakespeare contrasted 'Crabbed Age and Youth' in his couplet:

> Youth is hot and bold
> Age is weak and cold.

This, maybe, is an exaggerated polarization of identifying characteristics but it contains a strong element of truth. The gap is essentially one of age, accentuated by the rate and extent of change in the period involved. The speed at which change is taking place is constantly increasing and this naturally sharpens the contrast. Youth will always challenge established institutions and ideas and the traditional order of things to which their elders have become accustomed and accept as fixed and unchangeable. It is not unusual, either, for youth to be attracted to revolutionary ideas and movements. This challenge to the old and established way of life is the dynamic in any society at any time and without which there could be little progress. In the absence of such a challenge, society becomes atrophied and its social systems fall

7

into decay. There is plenty of evidence in the history of human society to testify to the truth of this.

Each new generation takes the process a step forward and this is as obviously true of my generation as it is of those that have preceded or followed it, except that each generation starts from a more advanced position and in face of more rapid change than its predecessor. The issues may change, but in general the old and the new generations are joined within this constant process. Conditions at the beginning of the first half of this century were vastly different from those at the beginning of the second half. Tremendous changes have taken place in the material conditions of life, in the techniques of production, in the nature of employment, and in the standard of living. Improved education and communications have made their impact, with the result that the mass of the people, and especially the young people, have a new concept of what life ought to provide – a new vision of freedom and liberty of the individual and of the rights of man. The most significant advance affecting the generation gap is the extension of human rights which has led to a greater sense of independence and freedom. More concisely, the new generation is far less servile than its predecessor. Because of this, their challenge is bolder and more open, its protagonists much less subservient and inhibited. The influences that weighed heavily on my generation weigh much less heavily now. Religious pressure then was greater and people were more disposed to pay obeisance to what was considered the superiority of the landed gentry and the rich, and to accept a feeling of dependence upon them for security of employment. The modern generation is thus far less hag-ridden by tradition, and it is not surprising that they are far more aggressive in expressing their protests against outworn conventions and their demands for progressive change.

But my purpose in this narrative is to try to describe the problems, experiences and achievements of my generation as they appeared to me. The reader will, I hope, be able to make allowances and adjustments that will undoubtedly be necessary to fit my experiences and this account of them into the general pattern of history, of which they can only be a minute part. I can only present a facet of history as it affected me and the environment to which I belonged. My scene therefore, is set in the Rhondda with the coal-mining industry there, and later with the pits and miners of South Wales, culminating in nationwide responsibilities and activities. But, for the greater part of the story, the scene would differ little if it was set in any one of the older industries of the country. Actual involvement in events is personalized, and in this sense the record becomes autobiographical. But the setting in the coal-mining industry and my personal involvement in it is not the important feature of the record; it provides the local colour only. It could just as well have been Liverpool and its docks, with a contemporary comrade-in-arms, Leo McGree, as the narrator; or the Clyde, with an old friend, Finlay Hart, telling the story; or in steel or railways, around the many colourful characters those industries produced during the same period. The men mentioned are equally representative of my generation and there are obviously many more whose experiences and involvement were not unlike my own, who reacted and developed politically as I did. Although their personal experiences would be different in detail, they arose from the same events and policies and gave rise to the same struggles and activities and around the same aims. We were together pursuing a common purpose in the working-class struggles of our period. I am writing, then, as a representative of my generation with a personal story to tell which may help to illustrate the problems faced, the actions undertaken and the results attained. In this context, my own development to a position of national leadership in the miners' union is incidental to the story; what is more important is the progress made by the people as a whole towards a better and happier social existence. In this sense I become a self-appointed narrator of a period of history which I believe I helped in a small way to shape and which in the following pages is portrayed through my eyes and experiences.

The generation with which I identify myself is roughly the age group which was too young to have soldiered in the First World War from 1914 to 1918 but old enough to have been employed in industry during the post-war violent struggles of 1921 and 1926. I was born in December 1903 and can clearly remember that day in August 1914 when I was coming home from school and saw the newspaper placard with the two fateful words 'WAR DECLARED' emblazoned on it. By the time it ended, four years later, I had started work in the coal-mine, and we had moved as a family from the outskirts of Cardiff into the Rhondda.

A generation is an amorphous mass comprising all sorts of individuals, a motley collection of human beings moulded by their environment and acting upon it both individually and collectively. Yet it is difficult to answer the question as to why individuals react differently to the same events. Or why it is that some individuals remain indifferent or passive while others become intensely active and involved in events which may materially affect all of them in the same way. Is it a question of personal chemistry, temperament, intelligence, home life or family background? More likely, I suppose, it is a combination of these and many other factors. Whatever the reasons, I find it extremely difficult to answer or to explain my own involvement in revolutionary politics, since there seems little in my early life or family background which could have stimulated such interests.

Chapter 2

Early Life

My father started his working life as a farm labourer, but marriage and family responsibilities compelled him to seek work in the pits where the earning prospects were a little better. Of his father, I know very little except that he migrated to South Wales from one of the English border counties to take up employment as an iron-moulder. He died when my father was a boy and his widow married again. Her maiden name was Davies and she was born and lived the whole of her life in the locality. My mother was born in Watchet, Somerset, and with her parents migrated to South Wales when she was only a few weeks old. Although coming to Wales from Somerset, her maiden name was a good old Welsh one, Evans. Her father, of farming stock, had crossed the Bristol Channel to become bailiff at the Pentwyn Farm, now the headquarters of the Whitchurch golfing fraternity. He, too, died relatively young, after being gored by a bull. His widow and my mother eked out an existence by doing the washing and ironing for the big houses in the vicinity. My mother continued to provide this service for the Pentwyn household following the death of her mother, until we moved from the outskirts of Whitchurch, Cardiff, to the Rhondda.

We lived then in a small cottage at the foot of the drive up to the Pentwyn farm. Father worked in the Cymmer colliery, Porth, and travelled by train each day from Taffs Well railway station, a distance of about two and a half miles from where we lived, which he walked to and fro each working shift. He always worked on the afternoon shift and the folk living in the village of Tongwynlais, through which he passed each day, used to say they could set their clocks by him, so punctual was he. He was an onsetter at the pit bottom, which, although a very busy job, was considered light employment. He had previously been a skilled

11

miner but an accident had caused him to lose one of his eyes. I only knew him as a one-eyed man. Following the accident, the injured eye had to be removed, apparently to save the sight of the remaining eye, and this caused him great distress. Years later, mother told us that this period, when he feared he might go blind, produced in him such a nervous state that for years he suffered from chronic asthma, but as his fear subsided and his confidence returned so his asthma abated. He commuted his claim to compensation for the disability for a lump sum of £100, and this, together with another £80 or £90 he received from a collection by the men employed at the pit, he placed in the Post Office as a reserve against the possibility of going blind. Collections at the pit were a regular feature and were organized by the local lodge of the union and the proceeds distributed among miners who had been idle for long periods due to accidents sustained in the pit. His Post Office reserve was not touched – but was added to when my brother and I started work – until the lock-outs of 1921 and 1926, when it was drawn upon to help keep us. He lived until he was eighty years of age and retained quite good sight in his one eye to the end. Mother lived until she was past eightyfive years of age.

Thus my childhood was spent with an older brother and younger sister in this family setting and in the early years in a semi-rural area. The family circumstances were poor, with father receiving only light employment wages and having to meet a relatively heavy train fare to and from work. The low income was augmented by overtime when he could get it and, on weekends when it was not available, by working on the local farm, and by the small income mother received for the heavy work of washing and ironing. We were in those days a typical family of the respectable poor, regarding assistance from the poor law as degrading and accepting our poverty as a condition divinely ordained.

Living in mainly rural surroundings, we were not directly involved in the conflicts of the mining industry. The Greenmeadow estate was quite near where we lived and the old Squire Lewis was given some respectful veneration by the local people, while his gamekeeper was regarded by us children as a blackhearted monster. I remember on one occasion finding a nest of pheasants' eggs and proudly taking them home for the table, but being made to take them back to the nest, such was my parents deference to the property of the old squire. Our environment was a lot different from that of the Rhondda and the other mining valleys. I have a vague memory of the Cambrian strike and the Tony-pandy riots of 1910–11. It is a sort of dark memory tinged with fear, for the local folk were apprehensive of the people from the valleys. The Cambrian strike arose through dissatisfaction with the payment to miners employed in abnormal places, where their earning ability on piecework could be drastically reduced. It led to the principle of a minimum wage being accepted and operated in such circumstances. The strike was long and bitter, with large numbers of both police and soldiers being drafted into the area. Pitched battles were fought between strikers and police and the Riot Act applied for a time. The stories of violence obviously made an impression on those living a distance away in the more peaceful countryside, hence their apprehension of the valley people. The strike did not affect the Cymmer colliery situated some two or three miles lower down the valley, or at least, I have no recollection of father being involved. I have a more vivid recollection of the terrible explosion in the Senghenydd pit in 1913, when more than four hundred men lost their lives. Our family trekked with other local people to the top of the Caer-philly mountain from where we could see the village of Abertridwr, at the top of a little cul-de-sac valley where the pit was situated. This explosion was one of the worst in the history of British coal-mining, a big area of the mine having to be sealed off and abandoned before all the dead could be recovered and brought to the surface.

Nevertheless, while, at such times of disaster, there was a lot of sympathy for miners and their communities, the more usual attitude of many of the people in Cardiff and the surrounding villages was to regard mining people as in some way inferior to themselves. Even in later years, it was necessary from time to time to remind them that there would be no modern Cardiff without coal and the people who mined it. To the majority of the Welsh miners, the game of rugby is either a second religion

13

or a substitute for it, and when they descended upon Cardiff for the great international matches there usually followed a boisterous frolic in the pubs and streets. This caused some upset among those who considered themselves superior, more refined products of civilization and they voiced their condemnation in the press and elsewhere. There was a great deal of snobbery among these people and when the time came for us to move from these quiet country surroundings to the Rhondda, my mother, uncles, aunts and friends of the family were apprehensive. Going to live among miners and in the Rhondda they considered a terrible fate, a sort of irrevocable step towards hellfire and damnation, and we children were likely to grow up as heathens and ruffians, which was how they viewed the valley people. However, no matter how dire the risks, move we had to in October 1915, as father was no longer able to travel home at night because the late train had been withdrawn early in the war, and, although he tried lodging in Porth for some months, his wages were not sufficient to maintain two homes.

We moved into a terraced house in a small village high above Porth, which could only be approached from any side by climbing steep hills. The celebrated playwright and novelist Gwyn Thomas describes these gradients and the first attempts of buses to climb them :

'A local sage, Waldo Aberystwyth, gave the driver a most distracting tap and asked him if Rolls and Ford had been told of this particular gradient up to Trebanog before exposing humanity to this nonsense of internal combustion.

'To the left of the hills peak is the field where the rugby team from Cymmer and Trebanog used to play. It was the least level pitch in Christendom. Those who survived it got a diploma from Darwin. It was the only rugby field where the players were allowed to dip their bits of lemon in adrenalin while sitting in the oxygen tent at half time, and the referee was allowed to call in a relative or use a motor horn if he lacked the breath to make the pea move inside the metal.'[1]

[1] Gwyn Thomas, *A Welsh Eye* (Hutchinson).

14

Droll and satirical though this picture of the gradient and mountain top certainly is, it is pretty close to the truth. When buses first started this climb, I could begin walking from Porth as the bus started off and beat it to Tebanog by minutes. But there were great compensations for the gradients. We were up above the grime and dust of the pits in the valley with open country to the south. We were in a small community of people drawn together by a common interest in a single industry into which we were quickly assimilated. Like all mining communities, the people were warm and friendly, if sometimes rough and tough. Many years later, when age and health forced my parents to move from there, they were almost broken-hearted at having to leave.

I was around eleven years old when we moved into the Rhondda and I think of it as my real home; it was certainly the place where I spent my formative years, the oven which moulded me into the kind of man I was to become. Although I have lived in other parts of South Wales in later years, I have always considered myself a son of the Rhondda. In April 1965 I attended a meeting organized by the Civic Trust and the Rhondda Borough Council, held in the yard of the Cymmer colliery where I once worked, although then long since closed, to consider plans to erect a civic centre and beautify the whole valley scene. In the brochure published for the occasion, they described the Rhondda in the following terms :

'Both the Rhondda Fawr and Rhondda Fach are narrow, twisting valleys, where the rivers lie in a bed rarely more than a quarter of a mile wide, often with no flat bottom at all. The sides of the valleys saw the first coal workings in the Rhondda during the seventeenth and eighteenth centuries, when the outcrops were mined. During the first forty years of the nineteenth century came the first real industrial exploitation of the deep coal measures at Dinas. To a large extent this was, however, a solitary effort and it was only in 1849, with the arrival of George Insole at Cymmer, that the full industrialization of the Rhondda started. Discovery of the steam coal seam at Cwm Saerbren in 1851 led to the period of

15

peak activity between 1864 and 1894, and completed the transformation of the Rhondda from a quiet pastoral area to the most intensely mined valleys in the world.'

Not only was it the most intensely mined but also the most intensely exploited and many great fortunes were made by the early colliery owners from the richest and best seams upon which they concentrated. But the fame and greatness of the Rhondda rested upon its people; their cultural interests, in drama, music, education were wide and deep, as was their concern for the oppressed and persecuted. It was no exaggeration to claim that the name of the Rhondda was heard and known in the 'dungeons of the world, such was their traditional interest in national and international politics. It was in this environment that I was privileged to grow to manhood; in the pits manhood arrived quickly for the young lads who went into them.

It was possible to leave school at the age of thirteen depending on one's record of school attendances. I satisfied the test and left school at that age to work on a local colliery farm for five shillings a week and my food. Most lads who left school under this dispensation went to employment on the pithead screens, picking slag from the coal as it travelled over moving belts or tables *en route* to the trucks. I have no doubt that this special early school-leaving arrangement was designed to provide a source of cheap labour for this class of work – work formerly undertaken by girls and women, also as cheap labour.

I enjoyed working on the farm although it was hard and exhausting; a man's job, mucking-out cowsheds, helping with the feeding and milking, cleaning the stables and generally doing jobs normal to farm labouring. I think the experience helped to toughen me, and not only physically. Topping and tailing swedes or turnips on a cold and frosty morning does something more than merely test one's physical endurance. It requires a bit of guts, too. The most nerve-testing experience I had on this job, though, was having to walk each morning for seven or eight days to the top of the local mountain and to stay there until dark trying to spot a dog believed to be killing sheep. The mountain was flat on top with a pond in the middle surrounded by a bog.

Once over the crest, it was impossible to see a house or farm or any other sign of civilized life. A great sense of loneliness tinged with a certain amount of fear used to descend on me once I was over the crest, and I was in a state of near terror when, one late afternoon a thick mist, not uncommon on the hills, came down and blanketed everything, with visibility reduced to a few yards. I managed, however, to find my way to a farmhouse at the foot of the mountain where the farmer's wife gave me hot milk and food. Later, I spotted and identified the dog and the farmer had him shot.

Some people take work more seriously than others and I was obviously one of the serious types. On two successive nights after I first started on the farm I had nightmares. On both occasions I dreamed I was going to feed the cows; they were in overnight during the winter and it was my job to feed them before milking started. On both occasions I got out of bed and made for the bedroom window. The first night I got out of the window on to a sloping roof which I walked down but found I could not step off it into the back garden. The following night, my parents were on the look-out and stopped me before I got out of the window. We had lived for a few years in another house in the same terrace, where I could step up from the back garden on to the sloping roof, walk up it and get into my bedroom through the window. In the new house too great a drop between the roof and the garden prevented this. It was my first and only attempt at sleep-walking.

As I approached my fourteenth birthday, the age when I could work in the pits, I asked the farmer for a rise in wages. He gave me the answer I was to hear many times in the future, that 'he couldn't afford it', and in any case was selling the farm and moving to a new one a few miles away. Thus, the day after my fourteenth birthday, I started work in the pit.

At school I was not a particularly bright scholar and never reached top of the class, only once getting as high as third and on another occasion as low as twentysixth, but generally somewhere in the middle range. Despite this record, however, the headmaster at the Cymmer school did give me a letter to take home to my parents, urging them to allow me to sit an examination for secondary school. They would have made it possible had I wanted it but I was hell-bent on leaving school and starting work as soon as I could and, of course, additional money into the family purse was always needed and welcomed. So my formal education came to an end when I was thirteen and my entry into industry and hard work started. I went into the pits in December 1917, and began what was to be a lifelong association with the coal industry and the miners' union. I started as a collier's assistant, working at the coal face, serving an apprenticeship for a highly skilled job which required not only physical strength and courage but the ability to meet the unexpected and to improvize the means to overcome it.

This, then, is a very brief account of my early life and family background, with nothing remarkable or outstanding in it. In general it is the typical background of boys of my generation who had parents who cared and did their best for them, and who, although poor, were able to live in tolerable conditions, with just sufficient food and clothes and the occasional trip to the seaside to make life acceptable. It was the common background of boys and girls who left school as soon as they could to get into jobs and, according to where they were brought up, may or may not have had a choice of jobs. In single industry communities like the valleys of South Wales, there was little choice, so that boys usually followed in father's footsteps.

In the Rhondda, like Liverpool with its dockers, or the Clyde with its shipbuilders, we were the first or second generation of the migrant labour attracted to the new and developing industrial regions from the rural villages and towns of the four countries that make up Great Britain. Whether Irish, Scots, English or Welsh, we have much the same background to our entry into industry. The fathers of our generation came to the industrial regions from the countryside and brought with them the ingrained attitudes and inhibitions peculiar to the limitations of country life, many of them having their roots in the servility and oppression of feudal times but being carried with migrant labour to the industrial areas.

In 1871 there were only an estimated 33,000 mine workers in the whole of Glamorganshire. By 1891 the number had risen to 150,000, an increase of almost five times in twenty years. Much of this increase, around 50 per cent, came from beyond the borders of Glamorganshire; in fact, 37 per cent, came from the counties of Cornwall, Devon, Somerset and Gloucestershire. All this particularly affected the Rhondda, with its estimated population of no more than 4,000 in 1861, increasing to around 128,000 by 1891, and reaching 163,000 by 1921. It is an unfortunate and tragic fact that this speed of growth in South Wales, and particularly in the Rhondda, has in recent years been matched by the speed of its contraction and decline. The communities that grow up around extractive industries face calamity when the industry ends, unless there has been forward government planning of alternative industry to meet such a prospect, and to prevent such communities from becoming derelict. Effective plans have not been made to meet the rapidity of the coal industry's contraction.

I worked for the first year in the Coedely colliery which was situated a little outside the actual Rhondda valley. The pits were then working a six-day week of eight hours plus one winding-time each shift. The average winding-time was then more than half an hour, which meant on average men being down the pit for eight and a half hours each day. There were no buses or other transport to take us the two and a half miles or so from Trebanog to the pit, neither were there pit-head baths. On the morning shift, we were roused from bed at about 4.20 am to dress and walk to the pit, collect the pit lamp, and be down into the pit before 6 am. This shift would start to ascend at 2 pm which meant, with the uphill walk we had, getting home at around 4 pm. By the time we had got out of our pit clothes and bathed, more than twelve hours would have passed since we put them on. It was a state of affairs in which we were living only to work, with little opportunity for any other interests. Anyone's first impressions of working in a coal-mine are unlikely to be favourable; mine certainly were not. There were even one or two occasions when tears fell. On one such occasion, the man with whom I was working at the coal-face was obliged by the custom of the pit to take charge of a pit pony to haul empty trams into and full trams out from the working places. At intervals, he contrived to come

19

into the coal-face to help prepare coal for me to fill into the tram. During one of his periods of absence I accidentally caused my lamp to overturn and go out. I was 'in the dark' as they say in the pit. It is hard to describe this darkness of the pit. It is absolute blackness, impenetrable and eerie. Sounds appear to be magnified, the creaks of roof movement sounding like cracks of doom and the falling of loose pieces of coal from the front of the coal-face becoming frightening crashes, noises that are normal to the pit, heard and ignored in the presence of some light or company. The man and boy in the next working place could not hear my shouts and the tears came as I had to crawl in the darkness, feeling my way as best I could until they were able to hear me. The tears were not just because of the darkness, but getting 'in the dark' caused a delay in coal-getting for two sets of colliers, since a lamp had to be borrowed so that the one without light could be taken back to a depot, usually a good distance from the coal-face, to be re-lighted, and piecework earnings for both sets could be affected.

There was another occasion during the short time I worked at this pit when I was frightened. On the afternoon shift we descended into the pit at 2 pm, and came back up after 10 pm. I was able to walk half way home with my mate before he turned off for his own home. The second part of the journey was a continuous climb along a lonely, winding road with tall hedges and, at one sharp turning, woods on either side. I used to have to walk this last mile alone with only the light from the moon or stars, which more often than not were obscured by dark clouds. I reckon I was pretty easily scared as a youngster and lay no claim to bravery as an adult. The scare happened one night when passing between the two woods, I heard what seemed to be the clanging of a chain, and on looking back I saw a white shape moving between the trees. Tired though I was, I sprinted over the remaining distance, spurred on by fright, arriving home in a bath of sweat, alarming my mother by my agitated state. Walking to work past this same place the following day, I discovered the cause of my fright. What I had taken to be a ghostly presence was a chain-tethered billy goat grazing between the trees!

In South Wales, boys went straight to the coal-face when they started to work in the pits. They worked with colliers and in this way were themselves trained as colliers. In the Coedely colliery we were working on the Rhondda No 3 seam, about 2ft 6in. thick. The boy's job was to attend the collier and this meant 'running' with a 'curling' box. These boxes were large scoops holding, when full, up to about half a hundredweight of coal. The roof of this seam was hard sandstone and the floor soft shale. Consequently, height for the tram to get right into the working-place was made by cutting and blasting a roadway in the floor of the seam to the width and height of the tram. Running with a curling box in a thin seam involved putting the weight of the body on the hands, gripping the handles of the box and pushing the box forward from the toes with the body as near horizontal as possible. In this way, the boy could move at quite a good speed, so as to have an empty box ready at his mate's hands by the time he had filled the other one. The art in this work lay in being quick to find in the dark a foothold on the rim of the side of the tram before unloading the box; the hell of it was in ripping the skin off one's back when running by hitting against a protruding piece of roof; and the skill was of course, in learning how to prepare coal, holding underneath the seam, cutting through slips, understanding the grain of the coal, preparing and erecting roof supports, and maintaining road-ways – skills that have now been largely eliminated by the development of machine-mining.

I left Coedely within a year of starting there, and can offer no very conclusive reason for doing so, although it was most probably the distance and time taken up each day. I was able to get work with a collier in the Cymmer colliery where my father had always worked, where the seams were much thicker and where it was possible to work in an upright position, so that the work was a little less strenuous. By the age of sixteen, I was allowed to work on my own when my mate was absent; at eighteen, I worked on shares in a place of our own with my brother and later a friend, and before I was nineteen, I worked on my own, being accepted by the management as a competent collier. During this early period, although a member of the union, I took no interest in its affairs, but events were taking place which later

21

were to have a great influence in shaping my future and in stimulating what has turned out to be a lifelong involvement in the miners' trade union and in revolutionary politics.

Although my first impressions of mining were not favourable, I soon came to like the work and the comradeship of the men in the pits. In later years I often thought that if I lost the job I was then doing I would much prefer to go back to work underground than take a job on the surface, for I found coal-mining a very satisfying job.

Chapter 3

Years of Industrial Strife

Ours was a generation whose baptism into industry was in a world war and revolution. As we came of age for work the war was nearing its end. Although I had uncles and cousins in the army, some of whom were killed or wounded in action, no-one from our immediate family circle was directly involved, but we saw some of the physical mutilation resulting from it. As a youngster living in Whitchurch, I used to deliver the evening papers which I had to collect off the train and it was then I saw train-load after trainload of wounded soldiers being brought to the Coryton Halt (where I collected the papers from the train) with the mud and blood of the trenches still on them. Those borne on stretchers were still in their bloodied khaki uniforms, having been carried straight from the battlefields of Belgium and France to the huge mental hospital at Whitchurch which had been turned into a military hospital at the beginning of the war.

Towards the end of the war there were numerous revolutionary uprisings in Europe and revolutionary ferment was stirring in all the war-torn countries, including Britain. At the end of 1917, the workers of Russia had taken political power into their own hands and revolutionary governments had been set up in the Balkans and in certain centres in Germany, but they were short-lived, defeated by counter-revolution. In Britain, too, in the latter part of 1917 and for the next year or more, intense revolutionary ferment affected many parts of the nation. Strikes and threats of strikes were the order of the day. There was serious unrest in the army and near revolt in some of the naval bases on the south coast. In 1919 there was intense activity, particularly in dockland, against the British government's involvement in a counter-revolutionary war in Russia. It was a period when the main element in the government's internal policy was to buy time

23

by making concessions and other forms of appeasement. The Sankey Commission into the affairs of the mining industry was an example of this.

My recollection of this period is of the pit where I worked being flooded with discharged ex-miner soldiers from the army. In a working-place normally manned by a man and boy, and where they could not get the number of trams they were able to fill, three men and a boy were then concentrated. Thus we were idling for most of the shift, listening to the gory stories of the war as well as highly salacious accounts of fornicating interludes! Our wages were being paid, although output per man employed was never lower. From the standpoint of the government, however, it was an insurance against more serious revolt.

In January 1919, a miners' national conference decided to press for a 30 per cent increase in wages, and for the nationalization of the mines, with a measure of workers' control. The men, by ballot, strongly supported strike action; there were consultations between the partners in the Triple Alliance, the miners, railwaymen and transport workers, which had been formed for common action in defence and attack. Conditions were very favourable for a successful strike owing to an acute coal shortage in the country. However, the strike was not proceeded with for two main reasons: one, that the partners in the Alliance were not sufficiently enthusiastic and the main one, that the government proposed a full and free investigation into the affairs of the industry, and this was accepted by the union.

This ferment was equally strong in the political movement. In 1918, the Labour manifesto, *Labour and the New Social Order*, was without question a policy statement with greater socialist content than has come from this source since. Labour's revolutionary leanings at the time are manifested by the presence of Litvinov, a Bolshevik leader and statesman, as a special guest speaker at the Labour Party Conference, where he was given a tremendous welcome. By the end of that year, Labour had withdrawn their representatives from the coalition war government, and had agreed on a progressive programme: extensive nationalization; for a national minimum wage, for shorter hours of work; and for the right to work or receive full maintenance.

Throughout 1919 there were strikes in many industries, with the employers and the government on the defensive. It was potentially a revolutionary situation, with a disaffected army and navy, with masses of discharged soldiers out of work, many still with their wartime weapons, with industrial workers pressing both economic and political demands and the Labour Party identifying itself with a successful revolution in another land. It is not surprising, therefore, that the government of the day did what they could to buy time and peace until this situation abated and changed.

Against this background, the Sankey Commission was set up to investigate the mining industry, to delay a wage increase and to avert a strike. The Commission issued an interim report in March 1919, and recommended an immediate wage increase of two shillings a shift and a reduction in working hours for men employed below ground from eight to seven hours in each shift. Their final report in the following June advanced a majority recommendation for the nationalization of the mines with the workers in the industry to be given some measure of control. The government, in a letter from Bonar Law to the miners' union, confirmed an undertaking previously given to a deputation, that the government were 'prepared to carry out in the spirit and in the letter the recommendations of Sir John Sankey's Report'. The wage increase meant for me a rise from the fifteen shillings a week I had when I started to a wage of over £3 a week when I was a little over sixteen years old, such was the effect of this increase on the previous ones obtained. The improvements, however, were of short duration. Two years later the wages increase, and more, was taken away after a three-month lock-out; the seven-hour shift was taken away after a seven month lock-out in 1926; and the promise of nationalization of the mines made by the government in 1919 was not realized until almost half a century later. Capitalism in Britain thus skilfully and successfully negotiated the revolutionary rapids to reach more settled waters from which they were to marshal their forces for a decade of counter-attack. Although lads of my age could not fail to be aware of what was taking place, they could hardly appreciate its full significance. This was certainly true in my case. Interest

25

in such events was stimulated by the counter-attacks of the employers, which the next years provided in abundance.

The counter-attack on wages started in 1921, with the miners in the front line. A temporary agreement made in 1920 following a short miners' strike terminated on 31 March 1921, after the coal owners had posted notices on all the pit-heads over the previous month stating their new terms of employment which were to apply from 1 April. The new terms included very severe wage-cuts. The attack had been anticipated by the miners' union and again there had been consultation with their partners in the Triple Alliance; on this occasion joint action was agreed, which meant that, if the miners were attacked, the railway and transport industries would be dislocated. In the event, however, the two unions withdrew their agreement to take supporting action and the miners were left to battle alone. I remember this lock-out very well, and although I was then seventeen and took an interest in what was happening it was not strong enough to engage me in union activity other than attendance at meetings. It was during this action that I started to go to the mass meetings at which the miners' agent reported on the discussions taking place and the issues involved. The 1920 temporary agreement had given a wage increase which was related to output and fixed to outputs above an agreed datum line. It was not until years later when I read up the history of this period that I became a little clearer about the meaning of this particular term. I certainly did not understand the complicated background of the wages arrangements which preceded the lock-out, or fully understand the explanations being given at the time by the union spokesmen. There is a tendency for union officials, then and now, to presume, quite unrealistically, that ordinary union members understand complicated wage and other agreements. It was a glorious spring and summer that year, and we young people spent much of the time in sport and walking in the mountains. But our discussions, such as they were, centred on serious topics. The Russian revolution must have made a big impact upon us. Although we did not appreciate its significance at that time, we definitely supported it. We talked of revolution and saw it as the medium for social change. We were attracted to socialism much to the annoyance of our Sunday School superintendent. We even talked about stopping the pumps on the surface of the collieries as a means of bringing the coal owners to their knees, and, if there was one topic on which we were all agreed, it was the nationalization of the mines; we were united in our hatred of the coal owners.

In the mining village of Trebanog, as in most mining communities, the people could be separated into two main streams – those who went to chapel and those who did not. Most of my friends during this period were 'chapel boys', not because of any deep religious conviction but out of deference to our parents, in my case to mother, who was deeply religious. I went to chapel three times on Sunday, and Band of Hope prayer meetings and Young People's Guild on three nights a week. It was accepted as a duty and on more than one occasion my brother and I were called from cricket or football to attend such week-night religious occasions. In fact, a group of us young lads and girls became members of the chapel when we were about sixteen years old. We were pressured into this during a visit to the chapel of a 'hellfire and damnation' revivalist a short time before the lock-out in 1921. I suppose the evangelist had to get results in some way and we became rather easy additions to the number of converts he could claim to have made, in order, I discovered later, to justify the high fee he was being paid.

None of us had deep religious feelings, in fact we considered that Darwin offered a better explanation for man's existence on Earth than the Bible and as a class of young men in the Sunday School we were involved in many arguments with the resident minister on the subject. At one time we had a Christian Socialist as a teacher and when the head deacon discovered this, he forcibly ejected him from the Sunday School! I renounced my membership of the chapel following the 1926 General Strike and miners' lock-out and this caused my mother a great deal of anguish. I remember coming home from the pit one afternoon to find the resident minister waiting for me. I was tired, hungry, in sweaty pit clothes, and certainly in no mood for a discussion on religion. He tried his best to get me to change my attitude and return to the chapel. Finally he got down on his knees, pulling

27

my mother and me down with him, and prayed for my salvation. Mother started to cry and I became very angry, yanking the minister unceremoniously to his feet, telling him as best I could that I would never respond to such methods. He then told me the story of a similar experience he had had in another mining valley of a lad like me refusing God, and how on the day following his talk with him, while he was walking down the street, the minister saw men carrying a body from the pit. It was this young lad, who, in the minister's words, had 'rejected his eleventh hour chance of salvation'.

I recount this aspect of my background because, looking back, I feel it had an inhibiting influence on my personal involvement in the mining battles of the period. We were concerned with being considered respectable and well-behaved, not bad things in themselves, except for the snobbishness they created. To harass blacklegs or risk falling foul of the police was regarded as a blemish on the character. This artificial detachment from unpleasant events, plus a native shyness and reserve delayed, I am sure, my participation in the affairs of the trade union and in politics. I was intensely interested in both long before I plucked up sufficient courage to face family opposition and become publicly identified with activities that were not always popular.

To get back to the lock-out and its outcome. We were idle until the beginning of July and then went back into the pits having accepted big reductions in wages, although less than those demanded by the employers at the outset. Thus the attack on wages and conditions had started and was to continue throughout the 1920s. Two main factors depress wages and both were present at this time. First, there was the direct reduction in nominal wages, a reduction in the actual amount of money wages paid and, in addition, there was the reduction in the value of money wages because the rise in prices reduced their effective purchasing power. Both factors were present and by July 1922, wages had been reduced to about half of what they had been in the previous winter. In December 1922, the average shift wage in the mining industry was 9s 6d which included a subsistence allowance, compared with 6s 6d in 1914, while over the same period the cost of living had increased by over 80 per cent. The miners were thus worse off than before the war. Years later, I spent many hours reading the minutes of proceedings of the National Executive Committee, the Delegate Conferences, and the account of the meetings with government representatives. The record of the discussions during 1922 with the Prime Minister, Bonar Law, make depressing reading. The miners' leaders were pleading the dire poverty of their members, whose wages were having to be made up to a subsistence level, and this was true of tens of thousands of the lower paid men in the industry. Their pleas fell on deaf ears. The employed miner was almost down to the poverty level of his unemployed brother and neither the coal owners nor the government was prepared to help.

The workers in other industries fared little better. Following the defeat of the miners in both 1921 and 1926, the wages of all other industrial workers were attacked and brought down piecemeal. Within six months of the miners' defeat in 1921, wages for upward of six million workers had been reduced by an average of eight shillings a week. There were strikes of resistance in some of the industries as they came in for attack. In engineering, the resistance to cuts led to a lock-out which lasted from March to June 1922. But despite resistance, or more accurately because of its piecemeal character, the standard of living of working people was being ruthlessly reduced and hunger and poverty stalked the land. There was no united resistance.

In these circumstances, as could be expected, there was a fall both in membership and morale in the trade union movement. Defeat and wage-cuts are not good recruiting agents for trade union membership. The tendency for most of us then – very different from the attitude adopted immediately after the war – was for a fatalistic acceptance of this fall in living standards. Our protest was muted, and as Aneurin Bevan was wont to say, 'silent protest evokes no response'. By the end of 1922, I was a collier working a place of my own, slogging hard to make a few shillings over the minimum wage each week. The Cymmer pit, started by George Insole seventy years earlier, was a notoriously bad pit for piecework rates. The margin earned above the minimum wage was hardly worth the strain of the great physical

29

effort it required. Things were bad for my generation then but even so worse was to follow.

The second offensive against wages began once again with the miners first on the receiving end. On 30 June 1925, the coal owners gave notice of their intention to end the wage agreement then operating, bad though it was, and proposed further wage reductions, the abolition of the minimum wage principle, shorter hours and a reversion to district agreements from the then existing national agreements. This was, without question, a monstrous package attack, and was seen as a further attempt to lower the position not only of miners but of all industrial workers. It is to the credit of the individual unions and the Trades Union Congress that they came to the support of the miners, understanding that it was necessary in their own defence. They were prepared for action, although not going as far as a general strike, which would have paralysed the country. The government, facing this united front of trade unions, again played for time and gave a substantial subsidy to the coal owners to continue the existing agreements on wages and conditions for a further nine months. They were of course not ready then for a showdown with the unions and needed time to prepare their organization and counter-measures. As events later proved, by the end of the nine-month period they were ready.

Again the coal owners posted notices of their intention to terminate the operating agreement and announced their new terms, which were the same as those offered nine months earlier. Out of the discussions with other unions and within the TUC the miners were assured of full support, this time by a general strike called by the unions affiliated to the TUC and with that body's full blessing.

May 1st, 1926 is one of the greatest days in working-class history in Britain. It saw for the first time action taken by a united trade union movement – action which was the most decisive ever taken against capitalism in Britain, with millions of workers taking part in a general strike in defence of one of their sections under attack; this was the political significance of the action. The General Strike lasted for nine historic days, being called off in the end by the TUC, not because the workers were

30

weakening but, tragically, because the leadership of the TUC weakened. They were intimidated by the government's threats of legal action. On 9 May, leaders of the General Council were announcing that some of them were to be prosecuted, or that the whole General Council was to be prosecuted. This was quickly followed by meetings between representatives of the government and the TUC; and the General Strike was hastily called off. There was a sudden capitulation of the General Council, which shocked the millions of strikers and certainly shocked the miners, who were now left to fight on alone.

The secretary of the miners' union was, at this time, A. J. Cook, an eloquent agitator, who coined the slogan around which all miners rallied: 'Not a penny off the pay; not a minute on the day.' Cook had been a union leader at the colliery next down the valley to where I worked and we heard much of his exploits there as a fighter for wages and particularly for pit safety. He later became a miners' agent for the Rhondda, and I remember discussing his work as an agent with the officials of the Cymmer lodge some years later, when I became a member of the committee. They supported his candidature for national secretary in 1924, but did not regard him as a good negotiator at pit level. He was, however, a master of his craft on the platform. I attended many of his meetings when he came to the Rhondda and he was undoubtedly a great orator, and had terrific support throughout the coalfields. He frequently said: 'When you hear that A.J. has been dining with royalty, he will have deserted you.' When he came back to Porth just after dining with the Prince of Wales, he was accused by the men at the meeting of having broken faith with them. These men were largely from the pit where he had previously worked and their accusations must have hurt him deeply.

The miners' lock-out dragged on through the months of 1926 and really was petering-out when the decision came to end it. We had fought on alone but in the end we had to accept defeat spelt out in further wage-cuts, the loss of the seven-hour day and the return to the eight-hour day. I finally got back into the pit in December 1926, with an experience behind me that was to lead to a decisive change in my life.

31

My Generation

This very brief account of the big industrial battles of the 1920s is given here because they dominated the scene during the formative years of my generation; they certainly exerted a great influence on me. It was an experience, I suppose, that demoralized many and made rebels of many others. The general affect, however, was defeatism, especially in leadership, with union membership falling by 1930 to little more than half its strength in 1920. It led to very weak resistance to the anti-trade union laws introduced in 1927, to break-away unions based on employers' patronage in one or two industries, to merciless exploitation of those in industry, and to humiliating poverty for the millions out of work. There was of course a sustained effort by the active political and trade union minority to keep the flag of resistance flying but it was a very tough task, as I was to find out when I became politically active a little later on.

Chapter 4

The Turbulent Twenties

After the lock-out, I went back to work on the night shift, which meant breaking contact with my friends who were on other shifts, and, because I found it difficult to sleep by day and was pretty well exhausted by the weekend, my way of life underwent a change. I became an addicted reader and had the advantage of the workmen's library attached to the colliery where a good selection of literature was readily available. I was able to get books out in the name of my father, my brother and myself. My old friend, Arthur Horner, acknowledged that the Cymmer workmen's library was the best of the many good ones to be found in the Rhondda valleys. Some can boast of being educated at Eton and Cambridge; for me it was the elementary school and the Cymmer library. I read with the aid of an oil lamp – we had not yet risen to gas or electricity in our village – and a dictionary, and meandered indiscriminately through a wide range of subjects before anchoring to political philosophy. I read through a great deal of the available literature outlining the philosophy of socialism as presented by the Social Democrats and the Marxists and found most satisfaction with Marxism.

As I stated earlier, I still find it difficult to give a positive reason for my gravitation to Marxism and revolutionary politics. Was it the hammering we had taken from the employers and the government that produced this reaction? If so, why had it not similarly affected thousands of others who had endured the same hammering? It was a period of naked class war with the working class suffering defeats, but I was not consciously aware of this at the time. Perhaps the bitter experiences had planted a seed that needed a few years of gestation before the revolutionary was born. I prefer to think that I was conceived from the marriage of

c

experience with study to become an active communist for more than forty years.

I actually joined the Party in June 1929, although I was a communist in outlook a considerable time before this. I attended their public meetings intending to join but found it difficult to pluck up courage to make the approach. I was also facing strong family opposition. However, there was a general election in 1929 and Arthur Horner was the communist candidate. I volunteered to help and became their main leaflet distributor in Trebanog! I had broken the ice and I joined immediately the election was over. It was not long before I was made secretary of the small Porth branch, given two paper rounds covering a very wide area, one to deliver the *Workers Life* on Fridays and the other, the *Sunday Worker* on Sundays.

At twenty three years old, I suppose I should have been caught up in the events of the General Strike and in the miners' movement, but in fact during the early weeks I was little more than a spectator of what were undoubtedly historic and dramatic moments in the history of this country. I can honestly state that I know much more about what happened during those nine days of the General Strike from later reading than from any experience or knowledge gained at the time – and there must be legions of my generation like me. I do recollect that when the General Strike was over, there were heated arguments among the older miners who condemned certain trade union leaders for capitulating. The name of J. H. Thomas, leader of the railwaymen's union came in for considerable attack, as did that of Ramsay MacDonald, then the leader of the Parliamentary Labour Party.

I and my intimate circle of friends were more directly involved when the soup kitchen was opened and became the source of each day's main meal. Both my father and mother were helping out in the kitchen. Money, of course, was in very short supply but father drew on his savings and we (that is, my brother and I) were given a couple of shillings each week for pocket money. The three of us had been working regularly throughout the years following the end of the war, except for the strike periods, and father's original savings had been added to. We were pretty broke at the end but, unlike those with young families to maintain, not heavily in debt. On such families the effect of the strike was really tough and for some remained a financial burden up until the second world war. Miners' wives in those days were housewives only and indeed in the prevailing conditions it was a full-time job. Even if work had been available to them, tradition and home responsibilities would have prevented them from taking advantage of it even in times of strike. Pit-head baths and canteens have perhaps been more of a boon for the miner's wife than for the miner.

As the miners' lock-out developed, I became increasingly involved and interested. We had a family of blacklegs in Trebanog, which caused not only bitter feeling in the village but gave rise to some activity, not always peaceful. The blacklegs were given police protection; otherwise they would have been stopped on the first day, for miners and mining communities hate and despise blacklegs. These single industry communities are so tightly bound by common interests and a deep sense of loyalty, that those who betray the common interests are immediately outcast, and are indeed lucky if that is all they suffer. The other aspect of this problem of blacklegging during strikes is that the people who do this are invariably inferior as workmen. Their weakness of character affects more than their sense of responsibility to fellow-workmen or their community; it is reflected in their attitude to work. I have a picture of three blackleg non-unionists in the Garw Valley in 1929 being escorted by a whole column of police. Usually, too, as soon as the strike or lock-out is over the employers find some reason to get rid of such men. They become a liability because other men shun and despise them, and of course, their value as strike-breakers has ceased.

Another kind of action which gave rise to local activity was the mining and selling of outcrop coal. Some men tried to sell the coal they produced from small mines driven horizontally into the side of the mountains. It was possible to find coal this way almost anywhere by penetrating the seams where they outcropped on the hillsides. This is now the source of vast areas of opencast mining. There was naturally a ready sale for all this outcrop coal; could it have been got away in the lorries that came for it in the dead of night, it would have been a highly lucrative operation for the producers. But getting it away was the difficulty and more than one lorry was overturned down the mountainside in an effort to discourage such activities. The nature of the terrain in the Rhondda made it extremely hazardous for lorry-drivers and it was not too difficult to stop such traffic in coal. Of course, obtaining a supply of coal for the home was a problem for all of us and while some favoured the outcrops others went to the colliery slag heaps. We got ours from this latter source, the three of us usually taking one day a week when we each of us hoped to fill a bag, which we then had to carry on our shoulders for a mile or more over the uneven and often slippery sheep-tracks on the mountainside. To get three bags could involve turning over twenty to thirty tons of slag which was hard work in any language.

Before the lock-out ended I was attending every meeting, particularly those addressed by A. J. Cook. The end came in a rather disorganized way, for the men rushed to the colliery offices to sign on for fear of not being taken back. It was a depressing but quite understandable end to the display of courage and fortitude. I was among the last to sign on again at the Cymmer pits and I paid for it by having to work regularly on the night shift and in a place where, as miners would say, the coal was as hard as 'the hobs of hell'.

There was a vacancy for a checkweighman at the Cymmer colliery and I was pressed into applying for it. There were several applicants, all of whom had served much longer in the lodge, but surprisingly I was elected in the second round of the ballot with over five hundred votes, the runner up having less votes in the second round than I had in the first. I was not yet twenty six years old, and truthfully was not really equipped to take over such responsibilities. The job of checking weights was easy enough, but it also entailed advising men on union matters and giving leadership. But here I was in September 1929, launched into my first official job in the miners' union, scarcely articulate, only able to stammer a few sentences at lodge meetings, with no experience whatever of negotiating with management, and regarded as too young 'a crot of a boy', as I was described by the elder statesmen of the lodge. I was in at the deep end and had to learn how to swim or drown, and it is on record that I did not drown.

Before the end of the year, the Mardy Lodge, of which Arthur Horner was then chairman, was in trouble with the South Wales Miners' Federation for having endorsed Horner as Parliamentary candidate in opposition to D. Watts Morgan, a former miners' agent who had been a miners' representative in Parliament for many years. The miners' leaders were recommending the expulsion of the Mardy Lodge and a delegate conference was called to decide this. The Rhondda lodges, however, arranged a meeting on the night of the conference without regard to what decision was reached and for a Mardy Lodge representative to be at the meeting. The delegate conference approved the recommendation of the leadership and the Mardy Lodge was expelled. We got to know that the miners' agents in the Rhondda were taking action to prevent the Mardy delegate from attending the Rhondda meeting and a few of us got together to try to see to it that the Mardy delegate got in.

We met the delegate, D. Lloyd Davies, as he came off the train and walked with him to the Porth miners' offices, which were in a sizeable square. We got to the offices to find a cordon of police stationed right across the office entrance, obviously to prevent the Mardy delegate from entering. Despite the police, we tried to get him in and this led to a scrummage in the office entrance. My recollection is of almost getting in myself but being stopped by a heavy hand pressing down on the back of my neck as I was pushing head first through the opposition. I got my arms around his leg but could not upset him although I tried hard. He turned out to be a miners' agent named David Lewis, who must have weighed more than twenty stone. Anyway, I was yanked out into the square by the police as our effort failed.

Following this little sortie with the police and while we were still gathered on the square, an elderly chap who was apparently supporting us had an attack of religious hysteria, and was pacing backwards and forwards across the square shouting religious verses. The right thing to do was to pacify him and not to excite him more, but a police sergeant started pushing him around and was, in my view, unnecessarily rough. I was naïve in such situations and went up to the sergeant to offer advice, suggesting that if he had to push someone around, why not try me. He was, of course, only too ready to do this and had probably been waiting for such an opportunity. I was ripe for arrest when the Mardy delegate, who seemed to know the sergeant very well, claimed that I was his son and that he would see that I gave no more trouble. Thus was I saved from arrest and from more serious charges than were subsequently made.

It was revealed later that the police had been called in to protect the office, and prevent the Mardy delegate entering, by the miners' agents who were really acting in defiance of a decision of the Rhondda delegates; at least this is what we were told by several of the delegates after the meeting. As it happened, the outcome of my first skirmish with the police was three of four summonses for minor charges and for which fines were imposed. The district meeting confirmed the decision of the delegate conference, although there was fairly strong opposition from some of the lodge representatives, and the Mardy Lodge was expelled from the South Wales Miners' Federation. This meant, of course, that Arthur Horner was also expelled from the union. He had been unable to attend the conferences being away on a visit to the Soviet Union. All the attempts to disband the expelled lodge and to form a new one within the union failed to break the loyalty of the Mardy men to their elected lodge leaders.

I was somehow fated during my initiation to politics to fall foul of the police and it was not all due to my own impetuosity. It can be said without malice that the Glamorganshire police at that time were being recruited more for their brawn than their brains. In fact, recruitment was almost exclusively restricted to ex-guardsmen, with the qualification related to height and not intelligence. The chief constable by background and inclination favoured strong arm methods. As Robin Page Arnot puts it in his first volume of the *History of the South Wales Miners*:

'Captain Lindsay had begun his career as part of the British Army of occupation in Egypt; and it may be that he never quite disabused himself of the notion that he was part of the Coalmasters' army of occupation in South Wales.'

In any event I seemed to be a fall guy for them so that when I was before the court in Marlborough Street, London, during the Hunger March of 1932, and the question was asked as to whether I had any previous convictions, a list of about fifteen including one prison sentence was read out. I am certain, too, that it was this record that earned me the maximum sentence on that occasion and not the actual incident which brought me before the court.

The Glamorganshire police were taking on the role of storm-troopers in the mining valleys of South Wales. Take for example the incident that led to my imprisonment. On 24 May 1930, celebrated then as Empire Day, we held a meeting in the evening in a side street off the main shopping street in Porth, for the purpose of exposing the colonial exploitation and brutal repression that the Empire really represented. The police came in numbers and tried to break up the meeting. We resisted by linking arms in a circle around the speaker, which they tried but failed to break. As soon as the meeting closed, however, they were able to get at us individually and one young lad was slapped in the face with some force. But there was little fighting and we moved away as peacefully as we could. The meeting-place was a traditional one where the Salvation Army and other religious groups regularly assembled. About a fortnight later, some fourteen of us received summonses to appear in court to answer over fifty charges in all. I had three, including one for 'indecent language' which was a complete frame-up because I did not swear, still holding strongly to my chapel upbringing. We considered that we were being persecuted by the police and called for a demonstration at the court on the day we were due to appear. Porth was the junction of the two Rhondda valleys and I was due to lead the demonstration in from the Mardy side and someone else from the Tonypandy side. There was no demonstration, only three of us, two with summonses to appear in court that day, and one elderly man. As we approached the court on a bridge over the railway line, we were halted by a cordon of police who were stopping all traffic including pedestrians. We discovered later that a big force of police had been brought into the town to stop any demonstration. When we replied to

39

police questioning by saying that we were going to the police court, they refused to allow us to proceed and pushed us back and I fell. On getting up, had I shown them my summonses they would no doubt have ensured my safe passage, but my reaction was to dash through the cordon and they failed to stop me. Between the cordon and the court were many more policemen so I was caught and, with arms twisted behind my back, was propelled to the court by two policemen. As we were going down the slope towards the court, I tried to escape and suddenly they both fell over my legs on to the muddy road. I made another dash for freedom but was soon caught again and this time was lifted completely off the ground and carried. I fought and struggled, giving up only when my trousers were in danger of being dragged off me. I did not know how many or who were the policemen carrying me, but I did know that I was being punched in the kidneys. I was being carried, stomach facing the road, with a policeman's arm round my neck and under my throat, so that my mouth was open as I gasped for breath. As we entered the police station, I was given a hefty punch in the mouth which smashed my upper dentures, scattering them to the floor as they dropped me. I know many people doubt the stories of prisoners being beaten up by the police, but this happened to me and later I saw it happen again in Bristol. In fact, when I was in the police station cell and heard the keys rattling to open the cell door, I immediately got up on the stone bed to be ready to defend myself, thinking I was in for another hiding; it turned out to be the police inspector, whom I knew, bringing me in a welcome cup of tea!

After an hour or so, they took me into the courtroom to face the charges for the Empire Day meeting and I tried to put up some kind of a defence. But without teeth and with lacerated gums, I was unable to make myself understood. A number of those involved in the incident were given gaol sentences, their cases having been taken before mine. I was only fined but was immediately taken back into the dock to answer charges for what had happened that day. I was charged with assaulting a police sergeant and two constables, the case being adjourned for two weeks with bail being allowed. In those two weeks, apart from having to obtain new upper dentures, I was involved in continuous discussion with the Communist Party on whether or not I should be represented by a lawyer at the adjourned hearing. There were those who felt we had a strong case against the police and with legal representation could make it stick. Others took the view that we could not expect justice from a capitalist court with or without legal aid, and this latter point of view was carried. I would have preferred legal aid, but as it was I had to put up the best defence I could and it was, of course, not good enough. The charge was violent assault on the police and I was sentenced to four months' hard labour for striking the sergeant a violent blow on the face, and two months for striking each of the two constables, both sentences to run concurrently. The police dominated these local courts which were rightly called police courts. The evidence, usually read from a little book or given from memory, was accepted without question by the magistrates. In fact, when we accused the police of telling lies, we were rebuked by the magistrate who explained that the police were accustomed to giving evidence to the court and knew the penalty for perjury!

I was taken back to the cell and later in the day, when the afternoon shift at the pit where I was checkweighman had descended, I was handcuffed to two policemen and taken to the train where I was locked in with them for the journey to Cardiff prison, a fitting escort, apparently, for one described by the police as a 'violent agitator'. My stay in gaol was uninteresting and I availed myself of the facilities for study. The first fourteen days of hard labour sentence in those days were passed in solitary confinement and without a mattress, which meant sleeping on a hard bed of wood.

I applied for permission to attend classes and was given three – first aid, European history and mathematics, which meant being out of the cell three evenings a week and being given a pencil and writing book. For the first month, the only reading allowed was the Bible and I brushed up on the scriptures. After the first month, library books were available and I read and tried to memorize poetry. The confinement did not trouble me at all, and I became an expert on sewing hems on new mailbags, and using them during the first fortnight to make my bed a little more comfortable.

I have been described in recent years as a 'powerful speaker' and even an 'orator'. When I came out of gaol, a social evening and reception was arranged at the Judges' Hall, Tonypandy. During the proceedings I was called upon to say a few words. I got to the front of the platform but when I started to express my thanks I became completely tongue-tied. I was clapped off the platform. On another occasion before this, I had been prevailed upon to take the chair in a local council election meeting. All I was expected to do was to introduce the candidate, a very good friend of mine, but I failed even to start and the candidate had to introduce himself. I used to get petrified before an audience and in the days preceding such an ordeal I suffered an acute stomach upset. I was not born with a 'silver tongue' and learning to speak in public was a long and painful exercise.

My job as checkweighman was kept for me and I returned to the pit towards the end of 1930, when another wage crisis was building up. We were facing a further wage reduction and there was growing unrest and opposition in the coalfield. At mass meetings, I was rising to my feet to say a few sentences but was unable to sustain an argument. Consequently, I was on and off my feet with these short outbursts much to the annoyance of the platform and of the meeting. Many were the threats to throw me out in the early days of the reports and discussions but as time went on I got enough support for the meeting to insist on my speaking from the platform. This of course made it more difficult for me, but I was improving. The outcome was a three-week strike in January 1931, and the end of my career as a checkweighman.

The industrial scene in the Twenties was vastly different from the scene today. Then, there was mass unemployment averaging a little under the one and a half million mark; the coal industry was badly hit, especially exporting districts like South Wales, through the Coal Reparations Plan imposed upon Germany in the peace settlement. By 1924 Germany's annual deliveries to France, Belgium and Italy were almost half the pre-war exports from Britain. The South Wales coalfield was ravaged by pit closures to cut back production. The pits in the northern ends of the valleys and the shallow pits throughout the coalfield were closed, with the result that mining villages and areas, later to be designated 'distressed areas', became derelict. Indeed, the 'rape of a fair country' has been a repetitive exercise against South Wales, and still is. Power, then, was with the employers and they directly attacked wages, starting as always by posting notices on the pitheads stating the terms of the new contract to replace the one coming to an end.

This was the position in the South Wales coalfield towards the end of 1930. On 30 November, notices were posted announcing that as and from 1 January 1931, employment would only be available on the new terms, and these involved substantial cuts The terms included a reduction in the minimum percentage addition to the base rates from 28 per cent down to 10 per cent; the bonus turn of six shifts' pay for five days worked on the afternoon and night shift was to be abolished (this was won in a coalfield strike in 1915); a reduction in subsistence rates and agreement not to recognize the National Industrial Board. These were the owners' terms and, coming as they did on top of the cuts imposed in 1921 and 1926, meant driving miners' wages down to a new low. The acceptance of such proposals could only mean that miners in employment were to be as impoverished and pauperized as those who were unemployed, ekeing out an existence on the dole. I spent the next weeks contending with and fighting against these terms, and against those who still found virtue in the dictum credited to Mabon of a half a loaf being better than no bread. This for me was the philosophy of defeat, which had to be fought if the cuts were to be resisted.

In the background to the discussions between the owners and union was the Coal Mines Act of 1930, introduced by the Labour government, which, among other provisions, repealed the Eight Hour Act and introduced a seven and a half hour shift to the pits, a reform that was supposed to apply from 1 December 1930. The coal owners put up a powerful resistance to this reduction in hours which was later amended to ninety hours spread over twelve work days. Another provision of the Act was the setting up of the National Industrial Board, which was to function as a conciliator in unsettled disputes between union and employers. It was presided over by an eminent lawyer with union and employers' representatives comprising the board. In this dispute, the owners were insisting that shorter hours had to be accompanied by reduced wages, and the Board recommended that the revised hours should be five shifts of seven hours thirtyfive minutes on weekdays, and a seven hour shift on Saturday. The owners were trying to determine both wages and hours settlements by coalfield discussions instead of national negotiatons making the latter ineffective by the introduction of coalfield settlements. In some coalfields, a fortnightly spreadover of ninety hours applied, in others the straight seven and a half hour shift for six shifts. Again, in some, the settlement included the acceptance of reduced wages, as in Durham, while in others, no wage reductions were imposed. In both Scotland and South Wales, there was initial resistance but it was not applied simultaneously, the strikes taking place one after the other. There was therefore no coordinated national resistance, and although a national conference had decided against the acceptance of the spreadover arrangement, it was adopted in some coalfields, even, for a short period, in South Wales.

There was no enthusiasm for the strikes among the South Wales leaders and this is shown by the nature of the argument between them and the owners during the strikes. Both agreed that the dispute should be settled by an independent chairman, but disagreed on his terms of reference. The union leaders wanted his powers limited to deciding the amount of wage reductions to meet the shorter hours, while the owners wanted him to have wider powers. Both were agreed that wage-cuts should be made, so that the dispute was really over the amount. Following intervention by the government, terms of reference were settled and the strike, which started on 1 January ended sixteen days later, it being agreed that the independent chairman should give his award by 28 February and that the wages rates applying in the previous November should operate pending the award. Mr F. P. M. Schiller KC was appointed, a man who had arbitrated in a similar dispute affecting the Bristol miners and had awarded a reduction of 2s 10d in the pound only a week or so before he

made his award on the South Wales dispute. His award announcement when it came opened with the ominous words,
repeated many times since: 'Having regard to the present financial and economic condition of the coal-mining industry in South
Wales and Monmouthshire I award. . . .' His award is worth
mention.

First, he reduced the minimum percentage on base rates from
28·5 per cent to 10 per cent; second, he amended the subsistence
provisions so that all unmarried adult, day-wage men whose
inclusive earnings were less than 7s 0d a shift be made up to that
amount; married adults with no children to be made up to 7s 3d
a shift; married adults with children to be made up to 7s 6d
a shift. Third, wilful absenteeism to be penalized by the forfeiture
of the subsistence make-up for the whole week of the absence.
Although the union leadership denounced this award, they recommended its acceptance but could carry their recommendation
in a delegate conference only by a very small majority. The union
statement pointed out that the award fixed the minimum wage
at 12·5 per cent above the 1914 standards but the cost of living
was 52 per cent above. It branded as 'heartless cynicism' the
subsistence allowance of 3d per day for a wife and 6d a day
for a wife and child, claiming that miners by this award had been
pushed down to a position 25 per cent lower than the average of
other workers. But no amount of denunciation could hide the
fact that its acceptance was a humiliating defeat.

Lessons drawn from this fragment of history could be useful
to the modern generation in industry. The first demonstrates that
sectional struggle, whether in defence or attack, is rarely effective. In this case, the owners were permitted to tackle each
coalfield separately and force district settlements on both the
hours and wages issues. The second is that strike action is likely
to be far more effective when it is simultaneous and united,
which it was not when South Wales and Scotland took action.
The third lesson shows that the division of miners into several
union organizations, although federated with the national union,
results in a serious organizational weakness. In South Wales, for
instance, craftsmen and winding-engine men were separately
organized, each conducting its own negotiations with the owners,

45

with the result that nationally, and within the coalfields, the unions failed to present a solid front in face of the attack. The position was aggravated, too, by the existence of the Spencer break-away union in Nottingham, and its off-shoot in South Wales, the South Wales Industrial Union, or, as we knew it best, the 'non-political' or company union, for both at national level and in the coalfield this break-away organization openly sided with the coal owners.

Another side issue emerging from the strike and the settlement of the wages and hours dispute which decisively affected my personal future concerned the new Communist Party policy and the minority movement which projected the concept of 'independent revolutionary leadership' by the Party, as distinct from its previous role as more of a ginger group within the labour movement. This leadership was to find expression in industry through the minority movement. The concept developed from decisions of the 5th Congress of the Red International of Trade Unions, to which the minority movement was affiliated, and was obviously the background to the creation of a Red miners' union in Germany and in Scotland at about this time. In the twenties, the minority movement had been a mass organization with wide support in the trade union movement, but after the General Strike it had dwindled in support and influence, as indeed had the whole trade union movement. In 1930 it mainly comprised branch affiliations and individual members and unofficial organizations.

In South Wales this new policy became the subject of rather bitter controversy, with Arthur Horner its most prominent opponent. During the hours and wages dispute, local and central unofficial strike committees had been set up with Arthur Horner as chairman of the central committee. The issue in the political controversy was whether the central strike committee should call for and lead strike action as an independent organization outside the trade unions. This obviously implied the creation of an alternative industrial organization to the trade union, which presumably would ultimately become an alternative trade union. The first act in this development was when the unofficial central strike committee called for a continuation of the strike contrary to the decision to call it off by a trade union delegate conference.

46

My own position in putting forward this policy will give an idea of what was involved.

On the Sunday following the delegate conference which had called off the strike, I attended a mass meeting of the members of my lodge and moved that we should continue the strike. I had a good hearing and the voting seemed to be evenly divided but, in the view of the chairman, my resolution was defeated. The same night, the other lodge secretaries and I reported to the leaders of the central strike committee in Judges' Hall how the lodges had reacted, which revealed that they had given a mixed reception to the decision to call off the strike. The committee decided that we should hold pit-head meetings the following morning for support of the strike. I did this at the Cymmer colliery but, during the meeting, the colliery manager with a dozen or so officials manhandled me out of the colliery yard on to Porth Square. The manager then shouted: 'In or out' to the assembled men and slowly they turned and proceeded towards the pit, leaving me on the road outside. This, it turned out, was the experience at most of these pit-head meetings; the men had been without wages for three weeks, they were going back on pre-strike wages, and there was, of course, always the forlorn hope of a favourable award from the independent chairman.

There was an aim beyond the fight against reduced wages or shorter hours; it was the much longer-term aim of building new unions through this conception of independent leadership. The issue in a nutshell, it seemed, was whether the fight should be to change the existing unions or to replace them.

I hold the view that the emphasis on militant policy must be directed within the unions towards changing policy and leaders where necessary, and that to concentrate on leading from the outside in unofficial movements may get some short-term sectional results but these are not likely to change the character and role of trade unions. In fact it is very often the easy road. It is a great deal more difficult to work for fundamental change from within a trade union than it is to agitate and build a sectarian organization on the outside. Anyway, Horner had doubts about the wisdom of the policy and argued against it, and I found myself supporting his stand. The issue became the subject of wide-

47

spread discussion with the Party and led to statements in the
Daily Worker. I felt there was a tendency to pillory Horner and
that the facts were more than a little distorted and I stated this.
The experience left me a little sour for a time.

The sequel to my attempt at 'independent leadership' came in
April, when I was summoned to the court by the colliery company for a breach of the 1860 Checkweighman's Act which laid
down that a checkweighman must not interfere with the management of the colliery. The lodge supported me and applied
to the Rhondda district of the union for legal assistance. Before
a decision was made, we were called to meet a small committee
where the miners' agent, W. H. Mainwaring, said I had been
acting on 'orders from Moscow'. The discussion became heated
and I walked out. However, the lodge officials remained and
legal aid was granted. The witnesses for the company included
the colliery manager, the colliery police sergeant and a fellow
checkweigher! In the face of the case law quoted against us, there
was little chance of winning, so we were not really surprised when
the stipendiary magistrate, of Tonypandy fame, and who had
been included in the Labour government's honours list a year
earlier, said he was satisfied there had been interference. He
would have to decide, he said, 'whether interference was sufficient to warrant taking away Paynter's livelihood'. He asked the
colliery agent and manager whether some accommodation could
be made, what sort of workman had I been and whether they
could give me a job in the pit. They said I was a good workman
and they would consider giving me a pit job as soon as trade
improved. Thereupon, he granted the company an injunction
for my removal as a checkweighman, telling me that a checkweighman on appointment had to give up some elementary rights
as a citizen and that his duty was confined to seeing that coal
was properly weighed. Trade did not improve and so I had
joined the army of the unemployed and was to share their fate
and problems for most of the thirties.

Years later, when I had become President of the South Wales
area, I frequently met in that official capacity both the agent
and manager of my old pit, the manager always claiming that by
removing me as a checkweighman he had helped me to get

where I was! Later when, as National Secretary, I was attending my last miners' delegate conference in Swansea in July 1968, Lord Robens arranged a surprise party for me one evening. He brought the old manager out of retirement to meet me and say a few words about our past association. As well as the manager, he also invited Gwyn Thomas, writer and playwright, who had signed on the dole with me although, because he had just graduated from the university, he got none, whereas I did.

So in a period of fourteen years we had three major lock-outs, each stemming from the workers' refusal to accept proposed wage reductions and lowered standards of living. Each time, the lock-out ended with the acceptance of worsened conditions, although a little better than those the employers had originally proposed. Each time, too, the employers had the support of the government of the day, whether Tory or Labour, although the Labour government from 1929 to 1931 was able to plead that it was a minority government and in that sense a prisoner of the other parties. During this period, like many others of my generation in industry, I had graduated from a passive participant in the confrontations to an active one, ending as a local leader at the Cymmer colliery, but only as a committee member of the miners' lodge, which in fact I became after being elected checkweighman. Then between September 1929 and April 1931, I spent a period in gaol and was removed from the committee for a short time. This was because I had supported a candidate in a local government election who was opposing the candidate supported by the lodge. In opposing the official Labour candidate, I had acted against lodge policy, but after a short suspension I was re-elected. Such a decision was of course outside the union rules and could have been challenged in court, but whatever our disagreements with union decisions of this kind, we would not seek to use the courts to settle them. In any case, this was trivial. My baptism was over; I emerged from it dedicated to the working class movement, a revolutionary socialist and an active member of the Communist Party.

Chapter 5

The Struggle Against Fascism

It is perhaps useful to comment on the rise of fascism in the interwar years and on its political content. During the 1920s, fascist organization and agitation grew so rapidly, particularly in Italy, Germany and certain Balkan countries, that by the early 1930s it had established political power in these countries. In Britain, fascism developed late, and, led by Sir Oswald Mosley, a renegade socialist, provoked fierce battles in parts of the country, but failed as a positive political force. In the late 1930s, the fascist powers formed an alliance, extended to include Japan, which was ostensibly aimed against world communism. Both in the period of growth and when it attained power, fascism was violent and ruthless, and at the same time demogogic in its incitement of people against communists and Jews in particular. It achieved power where the working class organizations of resistance were fragmented by internal divisions.

Capitalism has, for the last half century or more, been in a state of deep crisis. Two world wars are strong evidence of this, as is the birth and growth of an alternative social system over a large part of the world. Fascism and revolutionary socialism or communism, are both political by-products of this crisis. Fascism is a desperate political force keyed to defend and preserve capitalism when other less violent methods are ineffective. Its ultimate system of rule aims to eliminate democratic government and replace it with ruthless dictatorship which suppresses freedom and liberty. Although fascism can be found in many stages and forms, its main identifying characteristic is always the restriction or removal of the established freedoms and rights won by the people. When the preservation of capitalism calls for the restriction of democratic rights and freedoms, its defenders will not hesitate to enforce, by legislation or other means, the restrictions required. The political philosophy of fascism is not some new creed dreamed up by political fanatics like Hitler or Mussolini, but a product of capitalism in dire crisis, abandoning or limiting democratic government.

The fight against fascism in the 1930s was simultaneously a fight for peace, freedom and living standards. Territorial expansion to provide outlets for surplus capital and goods by peaceful means if possible but by force if not, is and always has been standard practice for a country trying to solve its problems at the expense of another.

Mussolini sought to expand by the conquest of Abyssinia in 1935 and later into Albania. Hitler sought to expand into Austria and arranged the murder of his fascist counterpart, Dolfuss, to facilitate this, and this as the prelude to the invasion of Czechoslovakia. Together they combined to overthrow the republican government of Spain by arming and financing General Franco and assisting with troops and officers. The fight against fascism was a fight against war and its extension into a second world war. It was a fight emasculated by the divisions within the anti-fascist movement.

The labour and trade union movements opposed the development of fascism in Britain and were concerned about its growth in other countries. In 1933, after Hitler had taken over power in Germany, the Trades Union Congress had before it a document perpared by Walter Citrine, the general secretary, entitled *Dictatorships and the Trade Union Movement*, which showed that the dangers of this development were clearly realized but that its political essence as a bastion of capitalism in crisis was not. The issue was presented both in the trade union movement and the Labour Party as *Dictatorship or Democracy*, which was also the theme of the speeches by the leaders in both organizatons, with opposition to all dictatorships whether of the right or the left, whether fascist or communist; the issue for them was 'dictatorship' and not its character and aims in relation to capitalism. Dictatorship in defence of capitalism is thus equated with dictatorship in defence of socialism. This was the state of confusion that strangled effective opposition, and which developed divided

51

and negative stands against acts of aggression perpetrated by the fascist powers.

The other main argument was based on the belief that fascism was the reply of the capitalists to the militancy of the workers, and claimed that if the workers refrained from militant action, supported moderation and were more accommodating in what could be described as a period of national difficulty, then fascism would fail and disappear. Fascism was thus presented as a subjective manifestation of force appearing in response to the use of force by working people. This kind of accommodation was attempted by the trade union and social democratic movements in Germany, but it did not stop Hitler from coming to power nor prevent him from throwing into prison the leaders who advocated such policies. Variants of the same political arguments are in fact the stock-in-trade of those in the trade union movement who shy away from direct confrontations with capitalism or action in defence of working class standards of existence, their rights and freedom. This is a continuing feature of the Labour movement in this country and is as great a source of confusion and disunity now as it was for my generation. How often have we heard the advice not to take part in some action or other, no matter how justified the aims, because communists are associated with it? Or to refrain from some action in favour of some more peaceful form of procedure because it was feared that conflict might incite reprisals?

In essence, this is the policy of accommodation, of seeking to modify the effect of some offensive act, rather than resist the offensive act itself. It was this philosophy of accommodation which divided the labour movement when Mussolini attacked Abyssinia in 1935 on whether or not sanctions ought to be applied. Those against argued that sanctions could lead the fascist powers into a war alliance, but as history was to demonstrate, it was the failure to stop such aggressive adventures that led to a second world war. The same kinds of argument were used when Hitler marched his troops into Austria and Czechoslovakia and again when the combined fascist powers promoted civil war in Spain. The arguments advanced by capitalist government to justify their policy of so-called non-intervention in Spain were the arguments used in the labour and trade union movements and which, in the most crucial phase of the conflict, were the basis of the policy adopted.

The classic situation which exemplified more than any other the political bankruptcy of this type of leadership, was the fascist-sponsored attack by General Franco to overthrow the democratically elected government of Republican Spain. Those who had previously argued that the issue was fascism or democracy now had their glorious chance of rallying to the defence of a democratically elected peoples' government. Such people, too, could now take action fortified with the knowledge that they were acting strictly in accord with the spirit and the letter of the Charter of the League of Nations and the Collective agreements adopted by the leading nations. But such people never act from principle, using only expedients, often shoddy ones at that. This was certainly the case in relation to the fascist attack in Spain.

The outcome was that both the TUC and the Labour Party supported the policy of non-intervention adopted by the Conservative government, and this policy was pressed by the British organizations within the Socialist International and the International Federation of Trade Unions. The propagators of this policy piously hoped that non-intervention would 'work fairly and be made effective'. It was well known and understood by those who pushed such policies, that Franco would never have attacked the Spanish mainland without massive military aid and that this was guaranteed by the fascist powers of Germany and Italy. The Republican government was thus starved of military supplies while Franco's aggressive armies were being equipped with the most modern weapons of war from the interventionist policy operated by Hitler and Mussolini. In these circumstances the labour movement became a supporter of the Government's policy of indirect aid to fascism, and although the policy was changed by later conferences, the change came too late and was too weakly applied to make any effective difference. It is a tragic story of prevarication and failure leading to catastrophe, the basic cause being a failure fully to understand capitalism in crisis and the political methods it will adopt to ensure survival.

Hitler came to power in Germany in January 1933, an event

that transformed what had been regarded as mainly a German problem into an acknowledged serious international one. The Mosley brand of the same cult had already arisen in this country and like others of my generation I was active in organized opposition to it. I was, however, privileged to give some small assistance to the German anti-fascist movement in June and July of 1933. The assault on the German working class was massive from the moment fascist power was attained. The principal leaders of the German anti-fascist movement were rounded up by Hitler's stormtroopers and were either murdered or tortured and imprisoned. This, too, was the fate of practically all of the national and regional leadership of the Communist Party. The organizations of the working class were without effective leadership and were shattered by the ruthless force of the attack. Some leaders in the early days believed that a policy of appeasement would save both themselves and their organizations, but their attempts at cooperation and their participation in the fascist May Day celebrations made no impact upon the Hitler régime and most of them were also thrown into prison.

I was in Moscow when Hitler came to power, having arrived there in December 1932. A little time previously I had attended a Communist Party school in Abbey Wood, Kent, which lasted for several weeks. It was at this school that I first came to know John Gollan, now the British national secretary of the Communist Party. He had arrived at the school straight from serving a prison sentence for distributing allegedly seditious literature to soldiers. After leaving the school he became the leader of the Young Communist League, and I was given the opportunity to continue my studies of political economy and social history in Moscow.

I left London on a Soviet ship in the company of a number of other students and we spent four or five days on a very interesting trip going through the Kiel Canal and up the Baltic Sea to Leningrad. It was especially interesting and exciting for me because it was my first sea voyage (unless one counts day trips on a paddle steamer from Cardiff to Weston-super-Mare as a sea voyage) and I was going to a socialist country. I knew enough about events in the Soviet Union since the revolution not to expect Utopia and my first sight of Leningrad was not inspiring. We docked at night, it was extremely cold and snowing, ice formed in the harbour had to be broken up by the ship, and the only humans in sight were Red Army soldiers muffled up to their ears in greatcoats. The next few months were spent in intensive study in conditions that were difficult in many ways. There was of course a language difficulty which restricted communication with the Soviet people. The weather was bitterly cold and after two years on the dole I was not equipped with the kind of clothing needed. While the food was plentiful, it was not what we were accustomed to and it took some time to get used to. During this period, I struck up a friendship with a fellow Welshman, Jim Cunnick, who had arrived there from Manchester where he was active in the Cooperative Society and USDAW. Looking back on this experience it is clear that we spent too much time indoors and it would have been better for us had we braved the elements more frequently. As it was, I had some English money from an insurance endowment policy that had been paid out just before I left Britain, most of which was owing to my parents who had been paying the premiums, and with this I bought a supply of drinks. Three of us sleeping in the same room had decided to relieve our self-imposed confinement with a booze-up. We must have made a terrific din before we passed out, and I know we were bawling rude parodies on some of the current popular songs. The outcome of this frolic was a special party meeting the following morning of the English-speaking group, where we were condemned and classified as 'petty bourgeois degenerates'. It was a pretty disgusting performance from any standpoint and poor thanks to our hosts who were doing their best to care for us. But my studies were really quite brief and I spent most of my time in what, for me, was a more interesting activity.

The Communist International, or Comintern as it was called, operated as a central coordinating organization for the national Communist parties. The Communist Party of Germany had been driven underground by Hitler and the Nazis and its leadership imprisoned or dispersed. The Comintern was anxious to do everything it could to assist not only the German communists but the anti-fascist movement as a whole. I was one among those who, following discussions with the Comintern, volunteered to act as a courier for financial and other assistance. I left Moscow for Berlin early in June 1933, proceeding by a somewhat devious route.

The first stage of my journey took me via Finland to Stockholm where I was to meet someone who would advise me upon the next stage. In the train journey through Finland, I had a rather interesting experience. At the Russo-Finnish border, a number of Finnish soldiers boarded the train and one young officer seemed to take notice of me, and was obviously interested in some copies of *The Listener* which had been sent out to me and which I was reading. He came over to sit by me and it turned out that he spoke very good English. He was interested in radio and explained that he was a radio 'ham' and had a regular contact with a radio enthusiast in Britain. He was aggressively anti-communist and pro-Hitler and I got the impression that he was a member of a Finnish fascist organization. He was curious to know what I had been doing in the Soviet Union and I pitched the tale that I was a mining engineer working for a British firm with a contract to install mining machinery, returning to Britain for a short holiday. He was very kind and took me to his flat in Helsinki, gave me breakfast and showed me his radio transmitting equipment. I have often wondered since whether this and other similar encounters during my travels were as innocent as they then appeared. When I finally arrived back in Britain, the Special Branch seemed to be well-informed about my movements.

Stockholm, where I had to stay for some weeks before I could move on, is a beautiful city and I spent my time wandering around it or lazing near the sea, enjoying a glorious summer holiday. But the time came for me to leave for Berlin and this was the part of the job that could be dangerous. I went from Sweden by ferry across to Stettin and from there by train down to Berlin. I booked into Lloyds Hotel, to find to my extreme dismay that the proprietor spoke fluent English and was an ardent supporter of Hitler. He claimed that a new equality between workers and their employers was being encouraged, and that in his establishment the servant girls now had their meals at the same table as he and his family !

I had been given an address at which I was expected to call

and identify myself. The means of identification was a small piece of notepaper torn in half. I assumed that whoever I was going to meet would have the other half. Of course, this all appears highly conspiratorial but precautions were necessary, since Germany, and Berlin in particular, were at that time anything but a haven of peace and rest for communists, and I was one, engaged in anti-Nazi activity. Berlin was a frightening experience with brown-shirts and stormtroopers everywhere. The people seemed in the grip of a hysteria which is hard to explain. In the streets, children and adults of all ages wore the swastika arm-bands, and lifted their arms in the Nazi salute on passing anyone, so that, in the busy streets in the centre of the city arm-raising was an almost constant motion. This salute was a must if one wanted to avoid being stopped and questioned, and I saluted like a robot – being anxious to avoid questioning. Almost every day one could read in the English newspapers of a foreigner being beaten up by fanatics for failing to observe some rite or other. I took no such risks for obvious reasons and spent heavily from my daily sub-sistence allowance in buying pamphelts whenever I was stopped by those selling them.

To get the address where I was to meet a representative of the German underground movement, I had to pass alongside the Alt Moabit prison where it was reported Thaelman and other leaders of the Communist Party were imprisoned. It was an ugly and depressing sight, with machine guns mounted on its high walls, and manned by stormtroopers, and a scene that did nothing to boost my confidence. However, I eventually reached the address which turned out to be a tobacconist's shop. I waited until the shop was empty before going in. Inside was an elderly woman and a young man, whom I assumed were mother and son. I handed them my piece of paper and they seemed startled and started a whispered consultation. The young man then came to me and ushered me into a small room behind the counter speaking to me in German, of which I was unable to understand a single word. He locked the door behind him as he left and I could only sit there and wait. Although I could not be sure, I had a feeling that these were the people I had to meet and that I was not being locked in to await a stormtrooper. When the door did eventually open, it was to admit a tall young man who came in with extended hand and saying *genossen* which I interpreted to mean 'comrade'. To say I was relieved would be an understatement. I was both relieved and delighted that I had succeeded in my mission of providing some aid to this representative of the underground anti-fascist movement. I was conscious, too, that any risks I was taking were as nothing compared to those he and those like him were taking every day. I could not then have known that the aid we hoped would help rebuild the anti-Hitler movement would not achieve this.

It turned out that I could not leave immediately and in fact I had to wait a couple of weeks before arrangements for my departure were completed. I met my contact every few days either in the tube stations or popular beer-houses, always where there were crowds, until finally he came with a suitcase which appeared to be full of technical books and I was able to book a flight from Templehof airport back to Moscow.

I made use of the period of waiting to do some sightseeing, visiting the Reichtag which had been burned down, and for which Dimitrov stood trial, confounding and defeating his accusers. I took trips out of Berlin to the beautiful lakes on the perimeter, Nicholasea and Wansea, and on one occasion I joined a tourist party to Potsdam to visit the palace of Frederick the Great. To get out of Berlin was to get free of the Nazi brownshirt nightmare, although meeting English-speaking tourists had its drawbacks too.

Because of the nature of my visit I was not able to make any significant assessment of the attitude of the German working class to the Nazi movement and policies. Hitler had smashed their organizations and his reign of terror effectively suppressed any demonstrations of opposition. In any case, I was unable to visit working class districts, and the people to be found in the streets of any big city cannot be taken as representative of the people of the country as a whole. If they could be, then the impression created would be of massive popular support for Hitler. I went by air from Berlin back to Moscow and must confess I did not feel really secure until I transferred to a Russian plane at Danzig.

I made several similar trips but never again to Berlin. I had some interesting experiences and on one occasion in transit and having to spend a night in Vienna, I witnessed a running battle between crowds and police in demonstrations against the Dolfuss régime and the presence of Hitler's advance guards in the country. However, the most difficult country to pass through *en route* to Moscow was Poland, where they carried out the most rigorous searches. On another occasion, when flying from Paris to Malmö in Sweden, the light passenger plane was forced down by high winds and the passengers, including myself, spent the night in a luxurious hotel in Amsterdam, where my private bathroom was bigger than any bedroom I had ever before slept in. It was on this trip too that I had encountered an English 'gent' who, while being obviously curious as to what a working man type like myself was doing flying from Paris to Malmö, told me he was flying to Malmö *en route* for a hunting holiday with the Swedish royal family!

A little sidelight, too, on the character of these Comintern activities concerns the allowance I was expected to exist on and which had a daily limit I could not exceed without giving a special explanation. So tight was the allowance that when I was returning to Britain from my final trip in January 1934 and was compelled to stay on in Paris to wait for a colleague who, it turned out, had been arrested in Switzerland, I had to borrow money from the person with whom I had made contact there. Again, on a previous occasion I had been instructed to buy a new suit which I did. It was a Paris tailor-made brown suit, and I needed it since I was looking more like a tramp than a respectable 'mining engineer'! When I left Moscow on what was my last assignment for the Comintern I was told to hand the suit back to Harry Pollitt in King Street and to request him to return it to them on his next visit. Being very independent, I carried out the instructions to the letter and handed the suit over to a very surprised Harry Pollitt.

The final incident in this brief account of my early involvement in the fight against Hitler and fascism occurred when I arrived home at Dover. I came in by boat from Calais, with very few possessions and certainly very little money. I cleared the passport check and customs without incident, and had boarded the train for Victoria when two men came running up the platform calling my name. Naïvely, I think now, I made myself known, much to their relief. They were quite ordinary looking chaps who told me that someone had been travelling on the continent with a passport similar to mine which could cause me difficulty if I had occasion to leave the country again, so could they check my passport. As soon as I handed it over, I realized their purpose, especially when they began to ask questions as they read out the places I had visited. I snatched back my passport, telling them to mind their own business and again boarded the train. They had obviously been waiting for me at the customs barrier but for some reason had missed me. Their interest in me, I have no doubt, was to confirm knowledge they already had from other sources of my activities during the previous year.

Chapter 6

The War in Spain

The struggle to defend and extend democracy is many-sided. We had our own internal battles in Britain against the growth of fascism. For two decades, this was a major threat to democracy and I have no doubt will be recorded in history as the great cause of our generation. The main strength of this spurious growth was outside Britain, although there were many inside the country who, with money and political support, did much to nurture it here and abroad. Mosley and his blackshirt army tried to build a political outpost for fascism here in Britain but could not. Big and violent battles took place in many parts of the country against his organized attempts to penetrate and provoke working class areas. Like Hitler and fascism in Germany, the blackshirt movement was violently anti-Jewish and perhaps the most fierce battles occurred in the East End of London and other centres where working class Jews lived and worked. In many places, however, the opposition of workers was too strong even for meetings to be held. I can recall a visit by a henchman of Mosley named Moran, who came with his van to Tonypandy. There was a spontaneous massing of people as soon as he arrived and he was forced to leave, but not before the angry crowd did battle with this blackshirt troop. Some thirtysix Rhondda men and women were sent for trial, many of them receiving gaol sentences, including a very close friend of mine, Harry Dobson, who was later killed in action during the battle for the Ebro in Spain.

In many areas, the struggle against the blackshirts created a great measure of united action among people of differing political outlook. This unity undoubtedly played its part in preventing fascism from succeeding in Britain, but perhaps the greatest single act that militated against its growth came from the fascist powers themselves. The attack upon the democratically elected government of Spain produced the greatest spontaneous outburst of popular anti-fascist feeling experienced anywhere. The campaign we conducted for support and aid for Spain and its people was the most responsive that I have ever taken part in; it was magnificent. It was much harder, however, to get support for political action from certain sections of the labour and trade union movement.

At the time of Franco's attack, in July 1936, I was temporarily installed as Communist Party organizer for Wales. The British Parliament went into its summer recess soon after the war started and the Prime Minister, Stanley Baldwin, left London to spend a few weeks at Gregynog Hall (just outside Newtown, Montgomeryshire) the magnificent home of the two sisters of Lord Davies of Llandinum, formerly a wealthy South Wales coal owner. The movement to aid Spain was calling for the recall of Parliament and demanding that the British government should change its policy and provide arms and other aid for the elected Spanish government, as it was indeed committed to do under the covenant of the League of Nations. At a point in this campaign, I received a message from Harry Pollitt asking whether I could organize a strong and as representative a deputation as possible to Gregynog Hall to press upon Baldwin the demand for the recall of Parliament. This had to be arranged quickly and within a budget of £12, which was all the money we had. I was able to muster a deputation of communist councillors, miners' officials, a shopkeeper who had a van and myself for the journey up to the middle of Wales. We travelled up, eight or nine of us, in an old car and the van, and arrived in Newtown where we booked into the local lodging-house. We aimed to get to Baldwin if we could, but in any event to get as much publicity as possible for the demand for the recall of Parliament. The wealth of the Davies family came from coal, Lord Davies being the head of the Ocean Coal Company, with several pits in South Wales. Gregynog Hall was in one of the most beautiful settings I have ever seen. We went into the grounds from the Newtown side, passed the lodge unchallenged and along a drive of great trees and colourful shrubs until, in an opening in the trees, on an expanse of green, we saw a mansion, white and grand, an ideal

62

place, I thought, for miners suffering from coal dust on the lungs!

We knocked on the front door which was opened after a while by a maid who looked a mite apprehensive when she saw us. We said we would like to see Mr Baldwin and were told that he was out for the day. Had she been a man, I have no doubt that we would have staged a noisy scene of some kind, but such a demonstration was not on when confronted by a little Welsh maid. We hastily scribbled a note which we asked her to give to Baldwin in which we stated our purpose and that we would call back the following day. We did go back next day but this time when we got to the opening in the trees we stopped not to admire the view, but because from behind the trees a number of men – plain-clothes policemen we later concluded – rushed at us, brandishing sticks. We were driven back and although we tried to take a picture of the charge, photography while resisting attack does not make for good results, and the picture was too blurred to reproduce. However, we got back to Newtown, held a meeting with the locals, and phoned the various newspapers and the BBC to give them the story, but the publicity our exploit received was disappointing.

As stated, the initial reaction of the labour and trade union leadership in Britain with some honourable exceptions was to support government policy, and to line up in defence of non-intervention. However, the pressure inside the movement was so great that before the end of 1936 this policy was modified, although the change was more of a formality than a reality. Aid for Spain committees were set up all over the country with a central committee at national level, and these committees did great work collecting and despatching medical aid, food and other essential goods. One of the outstanding features was the readiness of people to give what they could. We could go to the door of any unemployed family in the Rhondda and need only say that we were collecting for Spain and without question or exception we would be handed a tin of milk or a pound of sugar or whatever they had to give, and this week after week from the same homes. What was lacking was the political campaigning to bring pressure on the government to change its policy.

63

The campaigning was restricted mainly to left-wing organizations, and of these the Miners' Federation of Great Britain was in the forefront, and within that organization the South Wales miners were the pacemakers. The miners were solid and forceful throughout the whole tragic period, and there is no doubt that in the early days their powerful influence in the labour movement both at home and abroad was a major factor in changing the direction of Labour policy.

The British government was the main instigator of the non-intervention policy and it used political pressure on other European countries to join the Non-Intervention Committee of European Powers. I can recall some of the main arguments used at the time by those who supported non-intervention. Support for the legal government of Spain, it was said, could incite the fascist powers to attack other European countries and could result in large-scale war. As events proved, *their* policy led to a world war. There were others who held that it was a war between fascism and communism and why not let them destroy each other? Then there were those who believed that by non-intervention on the part of Britain and other countries, Germany and Italy would feel bound to honour a similar policy toward Franco. There were those of us, on the other hand, who saw this war as the opening shots in the fascist powers' attempt to conquer the world. These arguments, dressed up to meet modern circumstances, are in essence similar to arguments now being advanced to justify the hydrogen bomb, the war in Vietnam, wage restraint or anti-trade union legislation, and the contention that opposition on these issues if successful could give rise to something even worse.

It was against this political background – indeed, because of it – that thousands of anti-fascist fighters from all over the world went into Spain to fight alongside the loyal Spaniards. It was from this spontaneous surge of volunteers that the International Brigade was established and became the basis on which the British battalion was built. The government of this country really descended to the lowest of political depths in their efforts to stop recruitment to the International Brigade. Early in January 1937 they amended the Foreign Enlistment Act of 1870 so that it would apply to volunteers to fight in Spain. The Act provided penalties of up to two years imprisonment and heavy fines upon those who breached its provisions. Not only did they take action in Britain but they used their influence to get the powers in the European Non-Intervention Committee to follow their lead. Any kind of aid to the legally elected government was denied, and this was at a time when the press of the country was carrying stories of the build-up of thousands of soldiers and officers, tanks, heavy artillery, aeroplanes and other modern military equipment by Hitler and Mussolini. But recruitment, although now less open, continued and a steady flow of volunteers crossed the channel *en route* for Spain, erasing at least some of the shame that was Britain's, caused by the actions of its government.

I have no doubt that some day the whole story of the International Brigade will be written and its role in the Spanish civil war objectively portrayed, just as I hope that someone will soon collate all the records, individual experiences and anecdotes from the surviving volunteers of the British battalion, British literature and history would be enriched and posterity would learn more of this epic role undertaken by some men and women of my generation. My story of the Britons in Spain is only one of many that could be told, and is less interesting and certainly less dramatic than others because of the short time I was there and the nature of my function.

In March 1937, following the battles in defence of Madrid with the British battalion in the thick of them, the need was discussed in South Wales for a representative to go out to look after the battalion's interests at the International Brigade's headquarters, and to deal with individual and other problems. It was considered advisable to select someone with a trade union background and connections, and I was thought to have the necessary qualifications. I accepted but, I must confess, without any great enthusiam as I had got married only a few weeks before. However, once the decision was taken I proceeded to London where I was more fully briefed on the situation of the battalion and from there embarked for Spain.

The operation of the Enlistment Act previously referred to caused considerable political activity around the headquarters of the Communist Party and around those thought to be *en route* for Spain. I left London to get a boat from Dover to Calais; as soon as I got aboard, two plain clothes policemen cornered me and pressed me to give them the reason for my journey. However, they could do nothing to stop a young chap going to Paris for a merry weekend, which I gave as my reason! In an old yard in Paris, I was received by Charlotte Haldane who was in charge of the reception arrangements at that stage. The same night, together with a number of others, some from South Wales, we were put on a train for the south of France. Our destination turned out to be the town of Arles, although we saw very little of it, being billeted in a barn and only allowed to take walks after dark. We were given to understand that such precautions were necessary because the French government was officially against the recruitment and movement of volunteers through France, although the town council in Arles and the French authorities generally knew what was going on and tended to turn a blind eye to it. We were in the barn, sleeping and eating rough, for several days and nights and every day we could see that some had left and some new volunteers had come in. This was obviously the clearing house for the final move into Spain.

The time came for us to move on and we left in a car stopping only for a snack and a drink in Montpellier. From there we were taken into the country at the foot of the Pyrenees where we were met by two Spanish guides who had come over to lead us. We were given hemp sandals to wear, hanging our own boots round our necks by their laces, and, urged to make no noise, we started the single file upward trek over the mountain. Apparently we were not allowed to talk because we had to pass near an Army depot but in any case language difficulties restricted communication. Of the climb I remember the narrow goat-tracks, being given a drink of wine by an old man as we climbed, having a rest and falling asleep from exhaustion or excitement or both but waking refreshed for the remainder of the climb. We were having to climb with some speed because we had to complete the assault before daybreak, and this we were able to do.

Our descent into Spain was naturally much easier and quicker than the ascent and we made for the ruins of an old castle. Here we rested and were given food and drink before boarding lorries which took us to an army centre in an old Moorish fort in Figeurous. I was supposed to get to the Brigade headquarters quickly but my urgent pressure on the officers in charge made no impression whatever. While we were at this centre, we were given some elementary military training, route marches, learning to take cover, how to run under fire and so on. In fact it was the only training those who were going to join the battalion ever got. After a week or so, we entrained for Albacete and the Brigade headquarters. There I met Wally Tapsell, one time circulation manager of the *Daily Worker*, who had been Commissar at the Base, which was the impressive-sounding title of the job I had come to Spain to take on. Wally went up to Barcelona and was there in the early days of May when the Catalonian nationalists staged a *putsch* which was very quickly defeated by the loyalist forces.

I wish I had brought out of Spain the letters I received from Tapsell reporting the events in Barcelona, as well as copies of the reports that for the next months I sent back to the Party in Britain. As it is I have to rely largely on memory and the limited records now available. However, I wrote a letter to Arthur Horner which was published in the *Miner's Monthly* in its June 1937 issue, which gave my first impressions :

'Dear Arthur,
    'You have probably been expecting to hear from me before now, but the fact is, as you can well imagine, the state of things out here keeps a fellow pretty well occupied. The full story of what is happening to and with our lads out here will probably not be fully told until it is all over. This war, I suppose, has the same scenes of devastation, desolation, misery and suffering, that are characteristic of all wars. To those who are close to it, it is real and moving, and it appears more clearly not merely as a conflict of armies, but as a conflict in which masses of men, women and children take part.
    'To read the newspapers in England, one gets the mental picture of uniformed soldiers, the rattle of machine-gun fire, the hum of aeroplanes and the crash of bombs. Such is a very

incomplete picture. The real picture is seen more in the drab scenes, in the less inspiring and less terrifying aspects. To see twenty or thirty little children in a small peaceful railway station, fatherless and motherless, awaiting transportation to a centre where they can be better cared for, is to get a picture of misery. To see middle-aged and old women with their worldly belongings tied within the four corners of a blanket, seeking refuge from a town or village that has been bombed, is to get a picture of havoc and desolation. To see long queues of women and children outside the shops patiently waiting to get perhaps half a pound of soap or a bit of butter, is to get a picture of the privation and suffering entailed.

'Yet even this is not complete, because despite this, and as a result of it, you see the quiet courage and determination of the people as a whole. Is is a common sight to see the peasant farmer working in the olive groves or the ploughed field within the range of rifle or machine-gun fire; to see gangs of men right behind the lines who are tirelessly working to build new roads; to see men and women who remain behind in villages under fascist artillery fire in order to care for the wounded. Everywhere you see a people who by courage, self-sacrifice and ceaseless labour, are welded together by the common aim of maintaining freedom and liberty from fascist barbarism.

'Havoc and ruin caused by Franco and the combined fascist Powers, but over and above it, the unconquerable loyalty and devotion of the Spanish people to the cause of democracy. This is crystalized vividly in the events in Spain today. There is a section who would promote disloyalty and disunity, but they are substantially uninfluential and futile. The vast support for the new Government is proof of this. This section will be crushed, not merely in the formal sense by the Government, but by the invincible loyalty of the whole people. . . .

'It is here that you realize that a battle is in progress not merely to defend a people from a savage aggressor, but to destroy something that if allowed to advance will eventually crush the people of all democratic countries. . . .

From it all emerges one thing at least, and that is that the International Brigade and the British Battalion as part of it, is

not some noble and gallant band of crusaders come to succour
a helpless people from an injustice, it is the logical expression
of the conscious urge of democratic peoples for self-preservation. No-one would deny that the Brigade has had a tremendous and inspiring effect upon the morale and fighting capacity
of the Spanish people. Yet no-one would claim that it was done
out of pity, or as a chivalrous gesture of an advanced democratic people. The Brigade is the historic answer of democratic
people to protect their democracy, and the urgency of the need
for that protection would warrant an even greater response.'

These extracts from the letter reflect my political view of the
war and the deep feelings actual involvement in Spain aroused in
me. Even just wars are brutal and savage, and although they
give occasion for acts of great bravery, heroism and sacrifice
they also cause actions that are neither brave nor heroic but
unheroic and paltry. Both are human reactions to situations of
great urgency and difficulty. The men of the British battalion
were heroes who fought and suffered for a just cause and nothing
can ever be said or written to take that glory away from them.
And the same can be said of the nurses and doctors, the first
aid men and the ambulance drivers – all of whom worked tirelessly to help the sick and wounded. But in war and in a distant
land, no matter how politically conscious and dedicated the individual, problems and anxieties arise that cause distress and provoke uncharacteristic actions. I admit to acute anxieties of my
own while I was out there. Many of the men had left wives and
families, mothers or girl friends and there was constant concern
as to how they were managing. As there was no army maintenance allowance for serving in this war, the sacrifice embraced
not only the volunteer, but the whole of his family. My job consisted of trying to deal with these and many other problems as
best we could.

From time to time, because of political relationships within
the popular front government, there were difficulties in arranging repatriation to Britain, even of wounded men. There
were problems involving leadership in the battalion and the Brigade to which the battalion was attached, which did not arise

69

from political outlooks, but from personality clashes. This was a people's army where self discipline of a very high order was required and this, like every human quality, has its moments of weakness as well as its moments of great strength. The men of the battalion volunteered because they were politically conscious and wanted to help in the fight to defeat fascism, but zeal in support of any cause is a fluctuating subjective condition. Although it was my job to try to find solutions and remedies for such problems and difficulties, my own limitations and the limitations of the circumstances in which solutions had to be found, sometimes prevented their easy or successful achievement.

The battalion had been involved in heavy fighting in the early part of 1937, when the fascist armies had tried to cross the Jarama river, in their drive to isolate Madrid. The position was held and when the fighting subsided, both armies dug in and settled for a long period of desultory trench warfare. When I arrived at the battalion headquarters, it was to face very strong pressure to get the men out of the trenches for a rest and a break from the conditions they were having to endure. But withdrawing a battalion meant either putting in a replacement or thinning the whole line of defence, so that weeks passed, with several meetings with the International Brigade commander at the base in Albacete, before the withdrawal could be finally arranged. It was a short rest period, however, and had many drawbacks, being in a village with few amenities.

In July the battalion was moved to another part of the front at Brunette, to take part in an offensive aimed at reducing the pressure on Madrid. In the fighting, the battalion losses were heavy – in killed and wounded and in other ways. The ferocity of the battles, the absence of effective supporting arms after the first attack – they had been deployed to meet a fascist counter-attack on another section of the front – and the state of disorganization, all created problems of morale which led to some of the men leaving the battle front. A few found their way back to Britain, their stories being reported in the local newspapers, while others were arrested and brought to the prison in Albacete. It is fair to say, too, that at this time problems of battalion leadership contributed to this situation. It became my task to deal with the reorganization of the battalion and the release of those in prison. I got to Brunette five or six days after the big battle, taking with me parcels and letters from Britain. The position was pretty chaotic and the shortage of arms resulting from the policy of non-intervention was acute. The fascist tanks and aeroplanes which bombarded our positions daily could only be met with limited anti-tank resistance and rifle fire. I remember travelling along an old cart track in the van in which I had come from Albacete when the back door flew open and some of the goods fell out. I ran back to pick them up to find we were in range and sight of a machine-gun post whose bullets were kicking up the dust all around the lost goods, which had to be retrieved later.

The penalty for desertion is harsh in any army, especially in wartime. Together with reprsentatives of the American battalions, whose problems were similar to ours, we pressed the Brigade command to set up a centre where those whose morale had fallen could be rehabilitated. We emphasized, too, that military weakness in supporting organizations had contributed to the problem. Eventually the command agreed and camp was created where men in the same plight were brought together from the various battalions in an effort to rehabilitate them. I went to this camp with Arthur Horner and will never forget the experience. We had a meeting but the lads were not interested in anything Arthur had to say until he started to describe the Tommy Farr fight with Joe Louis. As for me, I had to talk my way out of a really difficult position and explain the problems of repatriation, the reasons for the camp and the alternatives they could have had to face had I not pressed for this camp, before their anger and bitterness subsided. In the end, after some weeks in the camp, most of these men rejoined the battalion refreshed and in good spirit.

We had a number of men from Britain down on the Cordoba front and we had been pressing for some time for them to be brought into the one battalion. In late July I had the job of taking a number of Italian volunteers down to the Cordoba front and bringing our own lads back. We travelled down through Spain in a big truck, sleeping and waking, breathing in the clouds of dust from the road, eating and drinking sparsely, depending mainly upon what we carried with us from the base. I cannot remember all the details of that tiring trip, but I recall going through the Ciudad Real, through magnificent country further south, eventually arriving at the headquarters of the southern command. Although the return journey with our own lads was much less tiring, the round trip took about five days and when I returned to Madrid at the end of it, I was so tired that although the hotel, where I managed to get a room only because it was within shelling range of the fascist lines on the outskirts, had its front porch blown off by a shell, I slept through it all!

In September the battalion was moved to a front around Belchite where a new attack was being developed. They were again in the thick of the fighting and the new battalion commander, Peter Daly, was killed. Peter was one of those who had been down on the Cordoba front and whom I had brought back to the battalion. I had some responsibility, too, for his being made battalion commander. He was typical of the men who were the backbone of the battalion as the short biography later shows. I was constantly moving about between the base and the front line and went up to the Belchite front to deal with problems following the casualties. I was travelling with a number of our men who were returning to the battalion, including Malcolm Dunbar, a fine man and soldier, who had just recovered from a wound in the neck. We were travelling along a straight road in a Ford van when we saw a big lorry approaching which, as it reached us, seemed to swerve. It hit us and we turned over several times before we came to a stop. Our driver fell out as the lorry overturned, I came out through the windscreen from the seat beside the driver, while the men in the back of the lorry took the full effect. The lorry-driver and I escaped except for a few cuts, but the men had to be taken to hospital at Benicassim. A heavy vehicle on a straight road with a tired driver was the official explanation for the accident. The following day I passed the same spot and found the van but it was pretty well useless for it had been stripped clean. There had been little activity on the Belchite front until this offensive, the positions captured providing some evidence of this. Behind the new positions reached by the Brigade was a well-fortified hill with well-constructed gun turrets and dugouts, the scraps of clothing lying about telling of women visitors. I was told that German officers had commanded this position and it would seem that creature comforts had been made available to them, but when I passed over the hill it was an upturned graveyard, with the stench of death from blackened bloated bodies testifying to the bloody battle that had been fought there.

I went out to Spain with the endorsement of the South Wales Miners' Executive of which I was then a member. I had with me a letter signed by Oliver Harris, the General Secretary, making official my trade union credentials, and this gave me some additional standing in the various negotiations in which from time to time I was involved. Elections to the executive committee took place every two years and one was due in November 1937, when it was considered advisable that I should return and seek re-election. However, although my work in Spain ended in late October, my work for Spain in Britain intensified on my return home. I was re-elected to the executive committee and attended meetings and conferences of miners' lodges all over the coal-field to report on the position out there. Without question, the highlight of those efforts came at the Trades Union Congress at Blackpool in September 1938, where I was put up by the MFGB delegation to second the following resolution moved by the ASLEF:

> 'This congress shall forthwith determine what effective steps shall be adopted by the entire trade union movement to secure a co-ordinated policy that has for its object the removal of the ban on Arms for the duly elected Government of Spain, as the policy now being pursued by the pro-fascist National Government is against international law and usage.'

Although the speeches of those who seconded resolutions at this Congress were not included in the congress reports intended for general circulation, they appeared in the copies distributed to General Council members and it was not until George Woodcock and I discussed this while we were both working with the Commission on Industrial Relations that I was able to take a copy of the speech from his volume. The speech was regarded at the

73

time as being out of the ordinary, not so much by its content as its effect. Apparently Walter Citrine, congress secretary, was expected to put forward the views of the General Council, but when the Chairman called upon him to do so, he did not respond. The resolution was put to the vote and carried by a show of hands, without the reservations of the Council being put to the delegates. I give here an abbreviated version of my speech :

'I feel that in seconding this resolution on behalf of the Mineworkers Federation I have a special capacity to do so, first because I happen to be one who has served with the International Brigade, and secondly, because I am a representative of the organization to which the General Secretary a few moments ago paid a very glowing tribute for its work on behalf of the Spanish people.

'It must be clear to every delegate in this Congress that the issue in Spain is one of which the outcome will not only determine the destinies of the people of Spain; it must be clear to everyone that the outcome of the conflict in Spain will involve the destinies of the people of all countries. . . .The conquest of Spain can well mean the commencement of further attacks upon other European democracies, and therefore I am pleading with this Congress that we should regard this matter not merely as one of solidarity, but as an issue of self-preservation for our trade unions in this country.

'In this Congress this week we have been facing the problems that arise in our factories and our industries. May I tell you that one of the biggest problems in the Spanish factories today is the problem of fainting. Working men and women are fainting at the lathes, at the point of production, because of hunger. That hunger is the consequence not merely of the attack that is being made by the combined fascist powers; it is the consequence of the encouragement and support that those fascist powers have received from the Government of our country. While we can pay our tribute to the heroism and self-sacrifice of the Spanish people, while we are confident that they will not give up without resistance one inch of their territory, or one inch of their rights, let us appreciate, too, that we cannot

74

expect the people of Spain to fight a combination that includes the Government of this country. That is our responsibility.

'I want to tell you of one experience which happened almost twelve months ago this week. I was returning from the front to a little town called Tortosa – a town that today has been completely demolished by aerial bombardment. On that summer afternoon as we entered the town we were confronted with the spectacle of women and children fleeing from it. Out of the air had swept a squadron of fascist planes. Their objective was to bomb a certain railway bridge across the river. The river was dry, and we were astounded to see some women with a terrible look of anguish on their faces rushing towards the river bed beneath the course of the aeroplanes. We were to learn the reason for their anguish. There in the dry river bed, playing in the sand, were between twenty and thirty little children and in less time than it takes me to repeat this story in this Congress twenty to thirty little children were blown to fragments on that summer afternoon. In the town of Tortosa there was not one anti-aircraft gun that the military forces could use to keep away those aeroplanes. The protection of that anti-aircraft gun was denied to those little children, not because there is an absence of self-sacrifice or heroism on the part of the Spanish people, but because there is too great a timidity inside the working class movement of this country in its actions against the 'National' Government, upon whom must be placed the responsibility for the deaths of those little children.

'The Spanish people are facing terrific odds. I have served with them as a member of the British battalion, and let us not forget in this Congress that in the British battalion are many hundreds who are members of the trade unions represented at this Congress. Many of them have realized that the war in Spain is a war that will eventually determine the destinies of their own kith and kin in this country. I want to plead with all the earnestness at my command, as one who has seen the terrible suffering in Spain as a consequence of the arms embargo, who has seen helpless people being murdered and mutilated without the means of defending themselves, as one who has lain on his stomach and seen the Italian aeroplanes above,

75

seen the silvery bombs being released, heard them screaming as they descended to the earth, and wondered whether it was his last moment on earth, and has deliberated upon the virtues of a supposed so-called non-intervention for which this Government has been responsible.

'In conclusion, I plead with the General Council and with the delegations of the various trade unions, that they will identify themselves in the localities, nationally and internationally, with any and every movement that gives us the chance to exert the maximum pressure upon this Government in order to bring about a reversal of its policy and greater succour and aid to the distressed people of Spain.'

Whatever the reservations of the General Council or of its secretary, Walter Citrine, he invited the miners' leaders, and the representatives of the union which moved the resolution, to detail the measures they would like the TUC to take. These were finally drafted by Lawther, Horner and J. R. Campbell and accepted by Citrine as the lines of action to be followed.

I was far too occupied and involved in my work to have made any useful assessment of the political situation within Republican Spain during the war period. The popular front government was made up of liberals, socialists and communists, and it is obvious that while such a coalition could be united in resistance to fascism, there could be differences on strategy and tactics, and more so on policies for reform within the country. From time to time, one heard hints of sharp differences on domestic policy, and on one occasion, on the role of the International Brigade. The leaders of the Brigade and those of the battalions were communists as were a big proportion of the actual volunteers, and there was obviously pressure from other governments against accepting aid from such sources. These strains and pressures were not helped by events in Catalonia during the first year of the war, where the anarchists' unions, the CNT, had taken over most of the industries, causing friction not only in Catalonia but within the government itself. Both socialist and communist representatives were for winning the war first and dealing with the internal problems afterwards. The liberal elements were obviously opposed to the revolutionary measures being applied in Catalonia; finally, steps had to be taken to regularize the situation so that the efforts of all could be concentrated on the war effort.

I remember that the train in which we travelled down from the Spanish-French border had 'CNT' stuck on the front of the engine. When the cigarettes, chocolates and other gifts sent out to the men of the battalion by ship arrived at the port of Barcelona as they sometimes did, I had to pay dock charges when I collected them. In May 1937, the position developed into an unsuccessful uprising against the central government, and apparently for the self-government of Catalonia. The situation obviously created serious distractions for the central government at a time when the maximum concentration was required for the main task of defeating Franco. I cannot judge the effect that these difficulties and differences had on the actual prosecution of the war, but any factors that disrupted internal unity were bound to weaken the total resistance. But whatever the internal weaknesses, the crippling limitation was the external embargo on the supply of arms and this finally resulted in victory for Franco and fascism.

During the months I spent in Spain, both Arthur Horner and Harry Pollitt visited the battalion. Both were popular with the men and were welcomed warmly. They came loaded with messages from home and information on what was taking place in the campaign for aid to Spain and other news that was not reported in the Spanish newspapers. Not only were these visits important for the men at the front but they were even more important for the wounded in hospital, as well as for the British nurses and doctors there.

Before leaving this brief account of the British battalion in Spain let me give a short description of the type of men who volunteered and whom I found good to know. There was Steve Nelson of the American battalion, who served through the whole campaign, and who, when he returned to America, wrote his account of the Spanish Civil War, published in 1953, just as he was sentenced to a twenty year stretch of imprisonment for possessing seditious literature, then Bob Thompson, who went back from Spain later to serve with the American army in the world war and to win their highest award, the Purple Heart, only to be refused a grave with the war heroes of America when he died prematurely. There was also Peter Daly to whom I was personally attracted both because he was Irish, and because he had worked for a short spell in the pits around Gorseinon, near Swansea. When only fourteen years old Peter joined the IRA and soon became a lieutenant. In 1922 he was wounded and taken prisoner by the Irish Free State Army. He lay in goal for seventeen months and was only released after maintaining a hunger strike for eighteen days. He later joined a Welsh regiment but he was discovered smuggling arms back to Ireland and had to flee there for safety. He died of wounds in the fighting at Belchite on the Aragon front. Fred Copeman, battalion commander through the Jarama battles, was one of the leaders of the Invergodon mutiny in 1931, when the sailors' pay was cut. Jack Jones of the Rhondda, who was forty years old when he climbed over the Pyrenees into Spain, was captured and imprisoned in Burgos gaol before being released after the war had ended; and Harry Dobson, with whom I had worked closely in the Rhondda, quiet and unassuming but a great comrade, who died of wounds on the Ebro in 1938. These are only some of the men whose background I knew personally, but they were typical of the quality of the men who volunteered from Britain.

A young friend of mine has made a study of the volunteers from South Wales.[1] There were altogether 170 volunteers from Wales, and 116 of them came from the mining industry, around 25 per cent of them union officials at pit level. Amongst them were leaders of hunger marches and three of them had led stay-down strikes against company unionism, the industrial form of fascism which raised its head in certain pits in the South Wales coalfield following the 1926 lock-out. The average age was over thirty and 18 per cent of the Welsh volunteers were married. The South Wales miners provided the largest regional occupational group in the whole battalion.

Many of these men were killed and in December 1938, a big memorial meeting was organized to their memory in the pavilion at Mountain Ash. Arthur Horner was in the chair but the guest of the evening was Paul Robeson who sang and spoke his tribute

[1] Hywel Francis, *Welsh miners and the Spanish Civil War.*

78

to the men who were being honoured. Thousands from all over South Wales who were present at the memorial pledged that fascism would be resisted, and adopted as their own the declaration of the loyal Spanish people and the International Brigade : 'They shall not pass.'

The Spanish Civil War could be described as a rehearsal by the fascist powers for the bigger war that was to follow. It was in Spain that they tried out their new military techniques. The *blitzkrieg* of intensive aerial bombardment and strafing was first operated against the Basque people of northern Spain. The resistance of the loyal armies was extremely strong in this part of the front and the intensive bombing was intended to break this resistance by physically destroying the towns and villages and by the mass destruction of the Basque people. It was estimated that one such raid, on 27 April 1937, killed 1,654 and wounded 889 men, women and children. The press correspondents on the spot reported that German planes dropped a 'succession of incendiary and high explosive bombs for three hours'. They described how the people were fleeing in terror to the west towards Santander, and how they were being strafed as they struggled along the roads. The estimated number of refugees created by this concentrated attack was put by those on the spot at 30,000, with around 50,000 being evacuated by sea. The name of Guernica, the small town completely obliterated by this murderous bombardment, will always be remembered with horror by those who can recall the terrible orgy of destruction that razed it to the ground and decimated its population. Some months later, hundreds of Basque children were brought over to this country and, as always, the South Wales Miners' Federation was among the first to volunteer assistance. A large contingent of the children was brought down to South Wales and housed in an old building in Caerleon made available by the local council. Immediately, a willing band of men and women was ready to care for all their needs and to provide constant supervision. Raising money from the people of the valleys was never difficult for a cause such as this. The miners' lodges, branches of all trade unions, street collections and donations from all sections of the community, assured the children's sponsors that food and clothes and their other requirements would be adequately catered for. Some of the older children were put to live with families who were prepared and could afford to keep them. A twelve year old girl came to stay with us and remained until she heard that her mother had arrived in France. But the miners' union was the main organization taking responsibility for the care of the children who remained in the region for a very long time, many of whom later rejoined their parents, some in London, others in France, and some eventually returning to their homeland. The young girl who had stayed with me until she rejoined her mother in France was there, I was later informed, when France fell to the fascists during the second world war. I often wondered what her fate had been until one day, years later, when I was President of the South Wales miners, we had occasion to meet some representatives of a research organization attached to the Monmouthshire County Council. One of them was a young woman who waited behind and introduced herself. She was the girl who had lived with us for a few months and who was now married to one of the research workers and living in South Wales.

Two other features of the aid given by the South Wales miners and in which I was personally involved arose from the aggression of the fascist powers. In 1938, when Hitler's armies were preparing to march into Sudetenland, which was part of Czechoslovakia, there was great concern for the socialist and Jewish population there. Representatives of the union visited the region to investigate the situation and to discuss it with the Austrian-based organization which was arranging the evacuation of people from the invaded region. As a result, a fairly large group of these people was brought over to South Wales and the union accepted full responsibility for their maintenance while they were with us. I was a member of the small committee charged with looking after them. We were able to find in Penarth a house big enough to accommodate them all. They were all German-speaking but wanted no truck with Hitler and were making arrangements to settle across the Atlantic, in Canada. They were with us for some months before leaving for their new country.

The other activity was far less public and consisted of giving aid to Spanish subjects on the run from Franco, and who had

fought with the Republican army. They usually arrived by working on tramp steamers which had called at a Spanish port. They
found their way to a Cardiff character named Meth Jones. He
had been an agent for the union but was at this time the general
standby at the central office. He would take their particulars,
contact various consuls in Cardiff, usually from South American
countries, obtain entry visas and then advise them of suitable
ships they could join for the journey. No-one knows the whole
story of what went on but we would often see Meth Jones in
earnest conversation with dark strangers, whom we assumed were
being helped on their way to a home that would be safer for
them than Franco's Spain.

Chapter 7

The Struggle for the Right to Work

Following my removal as a checkweighman I signed on at the labour exchange and claimed unemployment benefit. This was refused by the insurance officer on the grounds that I had been dismissed from employment for misconduct and I appealed to a Court of Referees. This court upheld the decision of the insurance officer, so I appealed to the umpire. My case was that I had not been dismissed by my employers, who were the colliers employed at the Cymmer Colliery. I was being prevented from following my employment, which was still available to me, because of an action taken by the colliery owners in securing a legal order which barred me from the colliery premises, and which if I broke could involve me in contempt of court. The umpire upheld my submission and I recovered the six weeks' unemployment benefit which had been withheld.

At this time I was very disgruntled and bitter with the Communist Party over the treatment of Arthur Horner and so dropped out of activity for a few months. I took up shorthand and in three months mastered and memorized the outlines, the gramalogues and phrasograms of Pitman's tutorial. I had ideas of going to sea and in fact I went down to Cardiff docks on a few occasions to explore the possibilities of becoming a seaman! But of course there were plenty of unemployed seamen and furthermore there was the difficulty about a card called the PC 5 which the applicant needed before being employed and which apparently was available from the seamen's union for the price of £2. It was unlikely that the seamen's union, led at that time by Haverlock Ellis who had broken away from the TUC, would facilitate the employment of a 'red'. The seamen I talked to advised me to jump a ship and I was assured that once the ship was out in the channel I could reveal myself and would be signed on. I not only lacked the courage to take that kind of chance, but the spirit of adventure was also lacking. In fact at this time the seamen were waging a big campaign against the PC 5 which discriminated against free opportunity for employment. A friend of mine, Len Jefferies, recounts his experience of holding a meeting at Cardiff docks to deal with this. The police were there, trying to stop the meeting, and when the police superintendent became annoyed he whispered to Jefferies that he had ways and means of dealing with chaps like him. Whereupon Jefferies immediately told the meeting what the superintendent had said. The men shouted their hostility and the police left. However, the speakers were summoned for causing obstruction and I can do no better than quote from the account Len Jefferies gave me of the court proceedings.

'I attended the Court early and requested a copy of the act and was told that the relevant part of the act was stated in the summons. I pressed for a copy of the act in full and was finally given it. As far as I now remember it was dated 1381 and I copied from it the most choice and nonsensical parts. I started my defence by wishing to draw the attention of the bench to the act. The Bench said they were only interested in the part that was relevant but I persisted and read only from the parts I had copied. Obstruction could mean 'breaking the battlements of Bridges, lighting fires in the roadway or leaving excretion on the road or pathway'. Never had the terms of this ancient act been so ridiculed. However, three of us were fined £2 each. We said we had no money and would therefore take the fortnight in gaol but they were not disposed to accept this. About a fortnight later they came first to Garfields Williams' place and started sticking possession tickets on his furniture which was to be sold to meet the fine. They later came to my place. There were three of them and I told them that any attempt at forceable entry would be met by forceable resistance, and that in any case the furniture belonged to and was

83

in the name of my wife. They said they would report back to
the court, but we heard nothing further. I did not pay the fine
nor do the fortnight in gaol.'

Police provocation was rampant during this period of mass unemployment and they were doing all they could to harass and
restrict the activities of militant leaders. It seems clear that, with
three million unemployed, they were apprehensive that a movement could grow to massive proportions and challenge the authority of the state. There is plenty of evidence to justify this conclusion in the experience of those of us who, in all parts of the
country, were engaged in organizing pressure for the right to work
and against unemployment.

By the middle of 1931 the economic and political situation
in the country was chaotic. A royal commission reported a desperate financial position and a commission was set up to report
and recommend where economies could be made. This was the
infamous May committee which recommended drastic cuts in
the main areas of social expenditure. The cuts were directed
against education, roads, pay and pensions and health insurance,
with a heavy reduction in health service expenditure, but the
biggest cut of all was in unemployment insurance, which
amounted to more than all the rest put together. The Labour
cabinet split on the issue of these economies, MacDonald, Snow-
den and Thomas deserting to join a National Government with
the Tories. Unemployment benefit was cut by around 10 per
cent so that a man and wife were dropped from 26s to 24s a
week and a single man from 17s to 15s a week. I retained my
membership of the miners' union through the years that I was
unemployed, but it was the National Unemployed Workers Movement that actively organized the unemployed, giving them service
when they were harassed by the 'not genuinely seeking work'
rule, and representing them at courts of referees. I joined this
movement and there was hardly a Wednesday or Friday, the
days when we were required to sign on to qualify for benefit,
when we did not hold a meeting, and it was this I believe that
helped more than anything else to turn me into a fair speaker,
but it took a long time. We became experts on the unemployment

The Struggle for the Right to Work

insurance regulations and the methods by which the punitive regulations could be sidestepped.

The immediate national action organized by the movement was a march to Bristol from South Wales to press the Trades Union Congress, the organization which represented the employed and possessed an economic power which the unemployed did not have, to fight against the cuts. But in addition to this demonstrations were taking place all over the country, many of them meeting with rough treatment from the police. I decided to take part in the march to Bristol and the experience did a lot to revive my spirits. The marches against the atomic bomb from Aldermaston involved roughly the same distance and days on the road as from Cardiff to Bristol. But generally speaking those who take part in demonstration marches today can afford to buy their meals and pay for any accommodation they may require. The unemployed who took part in marches during the thirties not only put their unemployment benefit at risk, they depended completely on the money they could collect *en route* to buy food and often boots and overcoats. We had to raise quite a lot of money before we could start to equip the volunteers with kitbags, blankets and other necessities, and the whole march with a lorry and field kitchen. This, however, while necessary for the marches to London was not so necessary for a relatively short journey to Bristol.

We left Cardiff on Saturday, 5 September for Newport, the first stop. This was a short trek but as always on such occasions the first few nights are sleepless for most marchers. Sleeping hard on the floorboards of a Labour Hall kindly lent for the purpose, rude jokes and noises from the boisterous lads, usually means that the second and third days out are exhausting ones. The march from Newport is always a trying one not just due to lack of sleep the night before, but more because of the roads from Newport to Severn Tunnel junction, narrow roads with the remote farm house or small hamlet which made marching so uninteresting and tedious so that we were usually glad of the change and rest when we boarded the train to get through the tunnel to Pilning, the first station on the other side. The journey into Bristol from Pilning is also pretty heavy going, but it is through residential areas

85

where it is possible to raise money. We reached Bristol around tea time and tea was provided by a committee of Bristol organizations. It was then arranged that we would march to the Horsefair, in the centre of the city, where we would hold a meeting. Thousands of unemployed in Bristol turned out to meet us and we were given a rousing reception. There had already been demonstrations against the cuts in Bristol and clashes with the police had occurred. At the end of the Horsefair meeting the South Wales marchers were told to line up so that we could go in an orderly way to the hall where we were to sleep. The chief of police told Hannington, the national unemployed leader, that we would not be allowed to march. This was obviously a stupid police decision since we were a hundred men and about a dozen women, all strangers to Bristol, and who would be unable to find the sleeping quarters unless escorted collectively. The force of this argument carried weight and the police chief agreed we could go in procession but without displaying banners and without a band. This was agreed to but subsequent events clearly revealed that a big police force had been mobilized to break up the march.

We had not proceeded very far along the street away from the Horsefair when there were shouts and screams. Those of us in the front who ran back to investigate found that the police had broken into the march at several points and were using their batons. A fierce battle developed with the marchers defending themselves as best they could. I went to the help of a lad struggling with two policemen and became involved with several others. I was carried into the police station in time to see the station sergeant delivering a vicious stomach punch to the lad I had tried to help. When the police carrying me released me on to the floor I stayed there, for it was inviting injury to stand up. We were searched and put in the cells, but not before we saw a number of others carried in, obviously having been mauled and roughly handled. We were later bailed out by local people to stand trial a few days later.

No marchers were injured, but, according to press reports the following day, so indiscriminate had been the police attack that several civilians were in hospital, one with a broken leg, and that newspaper reporters, had been on the receiving end of police batons. The Bristol papers blamed the police for the melee, and that I am sure tempered 'justice', for about six of us who were summoned got off with a fine. The court decision was certainly not in keeping with the kind of treatment unemployed leaders were getting up and down the country, where invariably the penalty was gaol. A deputation of six waited on the TUC but were refused admission or a hearing and were roughly handled, Wally Hannington getting a nasty gash on the head.

The demonstrations taking place all over the country were big and angry. As an example of one of these I cite the incident in Cardiff which again involved my friend Len Jefferies. They were holding a meeting on a piece of waste ground near Frederick Street as part of a plan to arrange a demonstration and a deputation to meet the Town Clerk to press for increased relief. The deputy chief constable and a force of police were at the meeting when the decision was taken to form a demonstration in the main street. Police evidence stated that Jefferies had said: "Come with me boys, we will line up in front of the Empire." "Then," said the deputy chief, "the crowd got out of control and I put up my hand to stop them." The police estimated there were seven or eight hundred people in the meeting and these were moving off to line up by the Empire. The police tried to stop them and a struggle developed.

According to police evidence Jefferies was on the floor underneath the deputy chief and the police used their batons to save the lives of Jefferies, the chief and another man. Apparently the price of having one's life saved by the police at that time was nine months in gaol because that was the price paid by my friend and others.

The evidence of the police superintendant was: "I knocked down four men with my fist, then took out my baton for my own safety and for those in the street." My own view of this and similar battles and from my own experience is that the police policy was to stop, by force, if necessary, any demonstration directed towards bringing pressure on the authorities responsible. The police were deciding what was freedom of speech and when the right to demonstrate was to be permitted.

A lot of printer's ink is used these days in bemoaning the violence which some people see as the main characteristic of the young generation. The violence associated with purposeful demonstrations seems more like a tea party compared with the battles fought in the streets of Britain between 1931 and 1936. I admit that the violence of a section of the young people today is not purposeful, but negative and undertaken apparently for its own sake and usually against other youths. My generation met violence with violence and suffered through the courts penalties far harsher than anything meted out today. I like to think that this and many other changes have been achieved because we stood up and fought.

In beginning this story I said it could have been written by Leo Mcgree or Finlay Hart, my contemporaries in struggle. In August, 1931, as we were getting ready to march on Bristol, Finlay Hart's unemployed shipbuilders were storming the council chambers in protest against the economy cuts, and six were arrested for rioting. All over Scotland, culminating in the great national hunger march of the winter of 1932, there were demonstrations and meetings which often led to arrests and imprisonment. It was difficult in those days to be an active militant and avoid being arrested on some pretext or other. On the Merseyside in September 1932, a big demonstration marched on the public assistance committee asking for an increase in relief to able-bodied unemployed, a supply of boots and clothes for the winter and a hundredweight of coal, together with the starting-up of work schemes. The committee was not unsympathetic and agreed to send a telegram to the government demanding the abolition of the means test. But as the demonstration was leaving the town hall the police interfered and conflict ensued a number of the unemployed being arrested. This caused deep resentment and in a subsequent demonstration meeting to protest against the action of the police, another battle developed. Birkenhead was the scene of running battles through most of the night.

The police afterwards arrested the whole branch committee of the unemployed workers movement and many others; forty-five were put on trial and Leo Mcgree and Joe Rawlins, two leaders of the movement, were each sentenced to two years gaol. Every town and industrial centre of the country was actively protesting against the economy cuts. Not only was there mutiny in the Atlantic fleet at Invergordon, but there was growing unrest within the police force and they too were holding their meetings even as they were attacking the unemployed.

The national employed hunger march arrived in London towards the end of October. I told something of its story in my earlier book. Many of the contingents had a much more gruelling march than we did from South Wales. The men from Scotland, the north-east and the north-west, were on the road for weeks longer. From South Wales we usually took around two weeks, following routes that would lead us into the bigger towns where local organizations were able to give us accommodation and feeding arrangements in their local halls. I was elected treasurer of this march, responsible for the collecting boxes and collectors. Our lorry and field kitchen was always ahead of us preparing the meals for our arrival at pre-arranged stops. We always had a courier riding ahead and reporting back the lie of the land. I recall that as we were approaching Bath he told us that the police would try to divert us from the main streets of Bath in taking us to our billet. We passed the word back, so that when we were stopped by the police, we gently percolated through them in the direction we wished to go. In fact, some of the lads with sore feet took advantage of the treatment the Spa provided.

In every place we stopped we were given a tremendous welcome and looked after in royal fashion by the committees set up to receive us, and in these committees, university students were always present in numbers. The one place where organization was absent, and this was due to its rural character, was Hungerford. Here we marched to its workhouse where we supplemented workhouse fare with our own food. Many contingents on this march fared badly in the workhouses they were forced to use, but we had few complaints. In Reading we were billeted in the cattle market, the only place available. Authorities were often hostile and if they could they made things difficult. For me the biggest thrill while we were on the road was when we came into Slough. Thousands of miners and their families had been driven from

South Wales by unemployment and many had found work in Slough; they came in thousands out on to the road to meet and greet us, some cheering and some crying but with open arms and hearts. Needless to say, there was much singing too. We arrived in Hammersmith, where we were billeted in the Labour Hall on the night of 26 October ready for the march into Hyde Park the following day. Altogether around two and a half thousand marchers, coming from all parts of the country, were billeted in the suburbs of London.

On the next day, Saturday, an exceptional mobilization of the police had obviously been organized to meet the march into Hyde Park. Special police were undertaking the normal police duties. As we marched in from Hammersmith, we had a line of police in front, behind and along both sides in pretty close formation. We were marching within a police box, and this was the experience of the other contingents. At least a hundred thousand people were assembled at Marble Arch to greet us. It is difficult to describe the feeling one had marching through this lane of cheering people, swaying and surging behind a wall of policemen. The intense emotion of their demonstration not only thrilled one's being but had a physical effect so that one's feet seemed scarcely to touch the ground. It was one of my most thrilling experiences. Fierce battles were being fought all through the afternoon while our meeting was in progress but marchers were not involved. I became involved as we assembled to march back to Hammersmith. I was arrested when getting the collecting boxes from our lorry and until the early hours of the following morning was in a cell in the Hyde Park police station. The following day the press reported the bitter fighting that had gone on into the night and which some suggested was due to fear and panic on the part of some special police who were neither trained nor accustomed to dealing with such situations. However, the whole of our activities while in London were affected by what had happened on the Saturday.

On the Sunday, we marched to Trafalgar Square and a meeting estimated at more than a hundred thousand gathered there. Again there were clashes and arrests. The big event was the lobbying of Parliament on the Tuesday night. A million signatures had been collected for a petition. Marching to Parliament was banned and marchers were advised to proceed there in groups but again there was police interference and groups were stopped and turned back or became involved in running battles. The Marchers' Council decided that I should be kept away from the Tuesday night activity to avoid the risk of a second arrest and I was taken by car to someone's house and kept there until it was all over. Several incidents had taken place since the Hyde Park meeting and my arrest there. The lorry and collecting boxes containing the money we had collected coming in from Hammersmith had been confiscated by the police and were held in my name. The leader of the Welsh march and myself had visited Earls Court, where he had been in the Labour College some years before, and while we were there had been taken into Kensington Police Station and held there for several hours into the night. The novel side of this arrest was that the policeman himself complained strongly against the cuts in his salary and the hardship he was suffering with an invalid wife. As we were being escorted, we tried to get him to come into a public house for a friendly drink, but this he declined, telling us we could go in. We did, thinking we could give him the slip by leaving by another door, but unfortunately for us there was no other exit. The policeman was one of those who had arrested me on the previous Saturday at Hyde Park, and since he was now in plain clothes, it seemed clear that he had been instructed to follow us. He told us that he had taken us in because he considered we were acting suspiciously! When he first met us we were standing at the bar of a public house near the old Labour College!

While we were being held at the police station we could overhear telephone discussions with the Home Office, and mention was made of Sir John Gilmour, the Home Secretary. After some hours we were allowed to leave, no charges being preferred. Earlier in the day I had been to the Hyde Park police station to press for the return of our lorry and collecting boxes, spending hours there awaiting a decision. It was made clear to me that prosecution for unlawful or riotous assembly was being considered and our property was being held pending a decision on this. In the event, however, and I believe because they had difficulty in getting the police inspector at Hyde Park police station to cooperate, no charges were made and our property was eventually returned.

During the following year, 1933, the agitation continued. It was clear that the temper of the movement was building up and pressures were forcing the more orthodox leaders and organizations to become involved. The government, too, realized that something had to be done if more violent clashes were to be avoided. In the budget proposals of 1934, they announced their intention to restore the cuts and introduce a new bill. The cuts were later restored but the bill as a whole strengthened the administration of the means test, creating more elaborate machinery for assessing 'means and needs' of the unemployed. In a speech following the publication of the bill, Aneurin Bevin described it as follows:

> The Bill is a studied attack on democracy. It perpetuates the means test, imposes concentration camps on the poor, deprives the poor of the right of representation and puts up barriers to progress.

The effect of the new act was to intensify the opposition movement. The fight was against poverty and hardship and the regulations of the new act created a condition of shared poverty by both the employed and unemployed through the family needs and means test. The employed were thus suffering an indirect cut in their earnings and making a contribution to the maintenance of unemployment.

While refreshing my memory of this period I read through back numbers of the *Western Mail*, a South Wales daily paper that is opposed to pretty well all the things I stand for. Things have to be very bad before they take up the cudgels on behalf of the oppressed, and in one of their January 1934 editions they complained that the Cardiff city council was being pretty heartless in their treatment of out of work people in arrears with rent. They cited cases and I quote three of them. Case A concerned a tenant at Ely who on 1 January was owing 6s 6d which on 8 January increased to 17s 6d. On Saturday, 13 January he was served with a warrant of distress. The cost of the warrant was 5s and a further 6s for the man in possession. The tenant paid 22s rent on 15 January. Case B again at Ely, with arrears of £3 5s, distress was levied and four men arrived with a lorry and seized his cabinet gramophone; this proved insufficient so they re-entered the house and took away a three-piece suite. Case C concerned a tenant incapacitated by an accident whose rent arrears were £6. In this case, the council applied for an eject-ment order. Thus the poor were being harrassed and hounded in their poverty. County Councils were getting tougher, too, in-cluding Labour councils. A school strike against the policy of the Glamorganshire authority started on 17 January and went on until 13 March in a small hamlet, isolated in the heart of the vale of Glamorgan with their school closed and the children expected to go to a school two and a half miles away. The County Council was prepared to transport them there in the mornings but expected them to make their own way home on foot after school over this distance of very lonely narrow country roads. After the strike they were transported both ways.

That same year we had a similar problem in Trebanog with the same County Council and the villagers elected me as the secretary of the parents' school strike committee. A provisional school for the under-eights had existed in the local chapel since about 1922. Trebanog was split between two education authori-ties, Glamorgan and Rhondda; one side of the road was in the Rhondda and the other in Glamorganshire both for educational purposes, and for parliamentary representation, and we wanted both authorities to join in providing an infants' school. Trebanog consisted of two streets, one fairly long and the other short and is situated on top of a mountain. While it was reasonable to expect older children to attend the schools in the valleys on either side it was unreasonable to expect infants to face the rigours of steep hills and prevailing high winds. The distance to the proposed school was about one and a half miles, but, as the local press described it, 'the road from Trebanog to Gellidawel is a lonely country one – little more than a path.' The County Council proposed initially that the children should walk both ways, but when the strike started on 3 September 1934, they provided a bus. It has to be remembered that there were no

93

school meals in those days and the children involved were aged between four and eight. The older children on the Glamorgan side were attending Rhondda schools and a financial arrangement between the two authorities took care of this. The strike continued until December and while it was on, we involved the members of Parliament, the local lodges and several county and local councillors. Because we would not accept the County Council's decision they issued summonses against the parents. We then withdrew the older children attending the Rhondda schools. The Council assured us repeatedly that they would put the application for a school to the Board of Education but in the end they revealed their own opposition by refusing the school because they considered that it was 'not justified'. The strike was called off early in December at a parents' meeting called during my absence in Cardiff, and the children were provisionally accommodated in the Rhondda school. Even this was an unnecessary hardship on infants, but it was in keeping with the general policy of cutting back expenditure in essential social services; and too many authorities in mining communities were collaborating in the attacks.

I returned from my travels around Europe towards the end of January 1934 and found a marked increase in attendance of both employed and unemployed at meetings and demonstrations. During 1931, when we were calling for some demonstration to enforce the demand for free or cheap coal for the unemployed, the response was weak. Just before I had left for the Soviet Union, I had led a march from Porth to the council offices in Pentre but only a hundred or so took part from a centre of over three thousand unemployed. Stopped by a cordon of police as we entered Tonypandy, we had to disperse and filter through to the council offices along the side of the mountain. Although our meeting with the police was without incident we were still brought before a court and fined, mine being paid by my father while I was out of the country. The operation of the means test in addition to the cuts was biting hard and creating resistance.

The year 1934 was one of intense activity for me. I was a leading communist in the Rhondda, but as developing speaker became involved in meetings and discussions throughout South Wales. The Rhondda was a pretty grim place with heavy unemployment, and although many pits were still working, the wages were low and there was plenty of visual evidence of the poverty and drabness of life. I can remember at about this time a young visitor from the Soviet Union came to us and I had to show her around. She was the daughter of Ilya Erhenberg, the famous Russian writer, and herself the editor of a young people's paper. I took her into the Pontypridd workhouse, and was myself shocked by the sights we saw there, especially by the plight of old people and unmarried mothers, the place was virtually a prison for these unfortunates, regimented and confined to the building as they were, suffering the most degrading and humiliating existence. I do not know what effect this sight had on our young visitor but it appalled me, for I had had no idea that such conditions existed.

But if the visual evidence of poverty was apparent in the Rhondda, it was ten times more so in the places I was now visiting for the first time, places at the top of the valleys; Merthyr and Dowlais, once with as great a concentration of industry as any in South Wales but now derelict; Brynmawr, Nantyglo and Blaina, the home of the Chartist Movement in South Wales, now ghost villages filled with workless people. I had not imagined that such poverty-stricken places existed. Industry had developed in these paces long before it reached the Rhondda. Both coal and iron ore were mined along the heads of the valleys and this provided the base for the great foundries and blast furnaces whose scars are part of the ugliness of the region, and which became the scene for Alexander Cordell's novel, *The Rape of a Fair Country*. The ruins of the old blast furnaces and early pits remained, together with the housing conditions of a century earlier. These were the 'distressed areas' of the 1930s, and it is not surprising that they were the centres of opposition to the means test and were always well represented on national hunger marches.

They were well represented on the hunger march of 1934 which was organized to demand the restoration of the cuts and the abolition of the means test. I did not take part in this one,

95

having only just returned from the Soviet Union when it started from Cardiff on 9 February 1934. When the marchers arrived in London and marched into Hyde Park, it was pouring with rain and, according to the headlines in one South Wales newspaper, police outnumbered both the marchers and spectators with an estimated force of between ten and fifteen thousand. On this occasion the marchers were able to get into the House of Commons to lobby members, and this led to a debate in the House on whether representatives of the marchers should be allowed to enter the chamber to put the case of the unemployed. This, however, was refused by the Prime Minister, Ramsay Mac-Donald. As previously stated, the agitation produced a new act which restored the cuts but perpetuated and strengthened the operation of the means test.

While the marchers were *en route*, both Tom Mann and Harry Pollitt were arrested for making alleged 'seditious' speeches in the famous Judges' Hall, Tonypandy, which I attended, but I heard nothing from either of them that I had not heard from other speakers, apart from their eloquence in putting their case. Some months later they came before the Assize Court at Swansea and were both acquitted. The case was based on shorthand notes taken by a policeman, and under cross examination by Harry Pollitt, he was forced to demonstrate his ability by taking down a statement which Pollitt read slowly. He failed to do so, having to admit that his shorthand was an improvised brand of his own! It was an exhilarating experience for those of us who had fallen foul of the police during this period to see them defeated and held up to ridicule.

The South Wales Miners' Executive Committee together with the miners' Members of Parliament met in a special joint meeting on 5 January 1935, to discuss the effects of the new unemployment act. They had before them a report prepared by Oliver Harris, the federation secretary, which claimed among other things that if the regulations of the Unemployment Assistance Boards were applied rigidly, the unemployed in the mining communities of South Wales would lose a million pounds a year in income. The report condemned the government's policy as the 'reason for untold hardship to thousands of families, the smashing

96

up of homes and the wholesale destruction of family life'. The meeting decided upon an 'all-in Conference' which was held on 6 January and attended by no less than sixteen hundred delegates. At this conference, some delegates demanded strike action, but the platform, whilst accusing the government of the most 'callous brutality', opposed such action, advising that this was a matter for the unions as it certainly was. The chairman, Mr Jim Griffiths, then president of the federation, argued when replying to the demand :

'We could have a South Wales Miners' Conference next week and call for a strike, but if action is to be taken why should it be merely a miners' action? If other workers had been as faithful as we have been there would be no need for this conference.'

The last sentence of course, referred to the miners and their communities always returning Labour members to Parliament. The plea 'Why miners alone?' is one not infrequently heard now by leaders under pressure from their members. The answer to such a question is that someone has to take the initiative to start and to take practical steps to encourage others to follow. However, this was the first of many such conferences which together created broad, united front organizations.

In the early days the committees excluded direct representation from the Communist Party and the unemployed workers movement, and although some Labour leaders would have liked to continue this exclusion, it was impossible because we were the acknowledged leaders who had been constantly agitating and organizing the unemployed and who could influence the trade unions, particularly the miners' union. There was, too, a division of opinion within the local Labour parties. For instance, the Labour chairman of the Merthyr public assistance board defended the new measures because, as he stated, some families got increases. He cited the case of one man who was given 3s 6d a week for five weeks because he needed boots and another who was granted 5s a week extra because of ill-health ! There were many Labour men, too, who had accepted jobs as assistance board inspectors – or means test investigators as they were called in the localities – because, so it was argued, they could administer the means test 'more humanely'! This, of course, was rather unlikely, but the effect was to create divisions and some weakening of the opposition movement. The united front committee embraced all sections of the community, whether political, trade union or religious.

Early in January 1935 twentyfour ministers from the chapels and churches of Merthyr signed a letter to the government deploring the harm that was being done by the means test. 'The few who are working' they wrote, 'are driven either to leave home or reduce themselves to the level of cruel poverty'. I had spent some time in the Merthyr area during a by-election campaign in 1934 when Wal Hannington stood as a communist candidate. The campaign was fought on the issue of unemployment and the need for new industry, and although Hannington lost his deposit, the campaign of meetings undoubtedly had a tremendous effect. The biggest meetings of the campaign were held by us, with Harry and Marjory Pollitt assisting Hannington, all extremely powerful and attractive speakers. I spent three weeks in the lower end of the constituency, living in an empty shop that was loaned to us, eating and sleeping rough, but organizing some of the biggest meetings the area had seen. All my life I had been told about 'Moscow gold' but have seen no evidence of it, in fact the Party was sustained in the main by the sacrifice of its members and its campaigns depended entirely on the money that could be raised as it developed.

On 4 February 1935 a demonstration of about a thousand women marched on the Merthyr area offices of the assistance board to protest against the cuts they had enforced through the strict operation of the means test. They were supported by around three thousand unemployed men. A deputation led by the unemployed leader, Jack Williams who later fought in Spain, was inside the offices putting the case of the unemployed when, it was alleged, some of the employees in the office provoked the women. This led to a mêlée in the office grounds during which windows were smashed, and several of the women arrested. The mood was such, however, that the women were soon released.

98

On 1 February the deputation appointed by the all-in conference met the Minister of Labour who promised to announce changes in the regulations on the 5 February. On Sunday, 3 February sixty thousand people demonstrated in the Rhondda – the press estimate and probably a conservative one. The chapels and churches abandoned their normal services to take part and all traffic was brought to a standstill. This was the scene in every mining valley. On 5 February, true enough, the Minister announced his proposed changes but these only aimed at reducing some of the harshness of the regulations and offered no real or fundamental change, and did nothing to reduce the increasingly militant opposition that was being expressed throughout the country. The kind of action described at Merthyr, and which later affected the Monmouthshire valleys, spread everywhere. For instance, in Sheffield on 6 February, the press reported that the Town Hall had been besieged by six thousand unemployed, nine policemen and a number of protesters were injured, and there were between twentyfive and thirty arrests. These demonstrations were demanding increased relief and were directed against both the assistance boards and the public assistance committees.

On Thursday, 21 March, such a demonstration took place at the top end of the western valley in Monmouthshire. It was organized by the unemployed workers' movement and was in support of a deputation to the public assistance committee whose offices for the region were in Blaina. The stories of what actually caused the ensuing riot are conflicting. The first reports said that when the Abertillery marchers were stopped by the police they agreed to disperse, and only reassembled when they saw the demonstration from Nantyglo, coming down the valley, being attacked. In the Assize Court held in the town of Monmouth later in July, police evidence reversed the story, stating that it was the Nantyglo men who had agreed to go back, not those from Abertillery.

The demonstration numbered around five thousand and the police force mobilized to meet it was led by the deputy chief constable of Monmouthshire, which in my view was an indication of their intention to stop the demonstration, by force if neces-

99

sary. The early press reports based on police statements said: 'Some difficulty arose and several baton charges were made. A number of demonstrators were rendered unconscious.' This rather laconic description is probably near the truth of what happened, that the demonstrators did not stop when ordered and the police used batons to stop them, not an unusual experience for us in those days. At the Assize Court the demands of the marchers were stated to be 'that the first 7s 6d of sickness benefit should be disregarded and that some allowance payment for rent and coal should be made to those seeking relief', not unreasonable demands in relation to the poverty they suffered.

The main charges against the leaders were 'riotous assembly', and 'unlawful assembly'. Mr D. N. Pritt, KC represented the marchers' leaders and during the proceedings he accused the police of memorizing the depositions of the case which had been written by the clerk to the lower court. The police statements were, he accused, word for word as written by the clerk, implying that the police witnesses had been given sight of them and had memorized them. Not unexpectedly, this was denied by the police and not accepted by the judge. Pritt's defence was that no advance warning by the police, as there had been in this case, made a demonstration unlawful, and that to prevent demonstrations was 'screwing down the safety valve', which could only lead to the kind of explosion that had in fact taken place. The essence of his case was that the police were assuming powers to determine what was meant by 'freedom of speech' and the 'right to demonstrate', a role being adopted by the police and by no means confined to Monmouthshire.

The outcome was that all those charged were found guilty and sentenced to periods of imprisonment ranging from four to nine months, the principal leaders getting nine months. One leader involved and sent to gaol was county councillor Phil Abrahams, a very able and well-respected leader in the community, whose nine-month hard labour sentence meant his immediate disqualification from the county council. I had discussed this possibility with him during the assize proceedings and we had agreed on the man to recommend to the local movement as his successor. This meant that I had to spend a great deal of time trying to rebuild

100

leadership and restore morale which had been temporarily lowered as a result of this savage treatment, and to prepare for the county council by-election. It was not just the loss of Phil Abrahams, but also of George Brown, another powerful local leader who had also been gaoled. Long periods of unemployment is of itself demoralizing and it is a tribute to men like Abrahams and Brown that the unemployed of Brynmawr, Nantyglo and Blaina were able to keep up the spirit of resistance.

During the years 1934 to 1936 my main activity was centred in Tonypandy, in the Rhondda, where the Party had its offices. We had four communists on the Rhondda urban district council and held many official positions in the miners' union lodges. From there we published an unofficial miners' monthly paper which had a fair readership over the coalfield. We struggled with the writing of articles and struggled even more intensely with the job of meeting the printers' monthly account! In 1933 the reorganization of the South Wales Miners' Federation had established the principle of a rank-and-file leadership in place of a leadership previously comprised almost exclusively of full-time officials. Arthur Horner had been elected a miners' agent in the anthracite district and was a powerful influence among the leaders of the union. In the Rhondda, too, the Communist Party published its own paper, the *Vanguard*, although we were comparatively small in numbers, we commanded an influence there and throughout South Wales that on many questions could be decisive.

Throughout most of 1935 and 1936 our activity against unemployment and its consequences was directed mainly through the united front bodies. Some of the miners' lodges took decisions for a one day strike, as did the Cambrian combine of lodges, but there was usually some difference between the left and the right within the combined committee which prevented such decisions being implemented. Such was the nature and the broad unity of the campaign that on many a Sunday evening we were invited to speak to chapel congregations from the pulpit, particularly when a big Sunday demonstration was in the offing. The whole period was a demonstration of the effectiveness of unity which proceeded not only a mass movement, but got results from the

101

government, which, although small, represented a little progress.

In July 1936, the Minister of Labour, Oliver Stanley, was replaced by Ernest Brown, who introduced a new unemployment bill that had apparently taken eighteen months to prepare and consisted of new regulations for the unemployment assistance boards. There were various estimates of the effect they would have; the Government claimed they would cost an additional three-quarters of a million pounds and would give some increases to about two hundred thousand families. This, of course, represented only a small proportion of the total unemployed drawing unemployment assistance. The South Wales joint unemployed council considered that the operation of the new regulation could have a depressing effect in South Wales. Aneurin Bevan expressed the view that between 65 per cent and 70 per cent of the claimants in South Wales would have reductions because the scales in operation there were higher than those proposed. Sunday, 26 July was the day of the biggest demonstrations ever. The estimate for the Rhondda was over a hundred thousand, the chapels and churches abandoning their services to take part. The press reported that it took over an hour for the demonstrators marching twenty abreast to enter the de Winton Field at Tonypandy where the meeting was being held. All traffic was at a standstill. The speakers reflected the united front and included Labour Members of Parliament and Lewis Jones, a Communist county councillor. There were similar gatherings in the other valleys; fifty thousand in Aberdare and twelve thousand in Pontypool, the press reported the following day.

Out of these massive demonstrations emerged the biggest march ever staged from South Wales, and one with the biggest and most united support. By then, I had been elected to the South Wales miners' executive for the Rhondda and had been sent in to the Taff Merthyr colliery area to assist in the union campaign to eliminate the company union established there. I was, however, with the consent of the executive committee, permitted to march and, in fact, represented them in it. It is as well to state here that although I was on their payroll at Taff Merthyr I was not paid for the period I was on the march,

102

contrary to the hints from some quarters. As before, the march was national in character but we were by far the biggest contingent this time, and with the broadest backing from the whole labour movement. We were over 500 strong and in the marchers' council were several MPs including Nye Bevan and S. O. Davies. Lewis Jones was the leader and I became the deputy leader. The march was really without incident except perhaps for the journey between Swindon and Newbury, when it rained steadily the whole day. We were drenched and our blankets in the kitbags were soaked. When we got to Newbury we were delighted to find that we were billeted in the Corn Exchange, which had hot water pipes around the sides where we were able to dry out our clothes and blankets. And to make things even more delightful, some benefactor treated us to a meal of fish and chips.

The march converged on Hyde Park on Sunday, 8 November and again the composition of the Welsh platform testified to the unity that had been achieved. The Speakers were Nye Bevan, Jim Griffiths and Bill Mainwaring for the Labour Party and Arthur Horner and Lewis Jones for the Communist Party. On the following day, a petition with a million signatures was presented to Parliament; the marchers' leaders addressed an all-party meeting there and won considerable support for the proposal that marchers' representatives should be allowed to put their case from the floor of the House. On 11 November, the petition we had delivered came before Parliament, with Attlee, then leader of the Parliamentary Labour Party, moving the adjournment to consider 'a definite matter of urgent public importance'. The motion was defeated, but not before a number of Welsh miners' members had pressed the case of the unemployed and forced a reply from Prime Minister Baldwin. A week earlier the marchers from Jarrow, led by Ellen Wilkinson, MP, had presented their plea to the government which had accepted it entirely differently from the way in which it received the national march. The South Wales marchers, it was said, represented a 'political agitation designed to discredit and overthrow the government'. Their own policies were discrediting them but the likelihood of their overthrow, however desirable, seemed remote even to those of us who wanted it.

Although permission to address Parliament was refused, arrangements were made for a deputation to meet the Minister of Labour and his staff, which meant that for the first time the unemployed themselves were able to put their views to a Cabinet Minister. The outcome was a set of new assistance board regulations which came into effect some time later, on 16 November. For me, the high point of the whole event was the march past the Cenotaph on 11 November, with the unemployed in striking contrast to the pomp and ceremony of the occasion. One of the marchers' leaders placed a wreath at the foot of the Cenotaph during a spectacle vivid with contrasts. Here was a royal occasion with a new king placing the wreath in front of one placed by the unemployed; the colourful Guards' battalions with their bright red coats and high busbies, following their bands, and a battalion of unemployed, representing the largest army in the country, in shabby clothes, with kit-bags strapped to their backs, but marching past with the dignity and poise of men who really were fighting to realize the world the soldiers whose death they were commemorating had died for, a 'world fit for heroes to live in'. It was a thrilling experience for those of us who marched past.

The great lesson of this march and the massive demonstrations that preceded it is that a united movement can arouse and attract the support of the people and that governments are compelled to take notice of the power that such a united movement commands and respond to the demands made. Although the unity was short-lived, it is on record as having eased the attacks upon the unemployed with a modification of the operation of the means test, a measure of success possible by no other means. It is a lesson that the present labour movement needs to learn and apply.

A strong feeling of adventure enlivened our activities during the early 1930s. This was as true of Liverpool or Glasgow as it was of the Rhondda. There was excitement and a certain element of danger in our struggles against unemployment and for better living standards, as my contemporaries in the socialist movement in other parts of the country will agree. As active leaders we were working harder and certainly for longer hours than when we were working in our respective trades. I used to leave Trebanog early in the morning for a two-and-a-half mile walk to the office in Tonypandy where I would remain all day except for meetings which might be anywhere in the Rhondda. I did a little lecturing in the evenings, sometimes for the National Council of Labour Colleges, with whom I had been a correspondence course student years before. I recall taking a class organized by the Ferndale miners' lodge on 'Leninism', a subject they selected. I used to walk from Trebanog to Ferndale and back five or six miles each way, to pocket the 1s 2d tramfare they would pay me! In some of these classes one found the 'professional student' who did little more than read and attend classes and avoided taking part in any movement but who could certainly make life difficult for the youngster just starting to lecture, as I discovered.

A schoolteacher friend had bought a ship's bell for our small Party branch in Porth which we used for street meetings. Three of us were really active there, Murray Williams, who later became the compensation secretary of the Lewis Merthyr miners' lodge, and Penry Jones, later the chairman of the Wern Tarw lodge. We fought local government elections with either Murray Williams or myself as the candidate. I recall standing for the Glamorgan County Council on one occasion against the sitting member who had been returned unopposed for many years. He was William Evans, head of the firm, Thomas and Evans, which produced the 'Corona' soft drinks and owned a chain of stores around the region. The Labour Party did not oppose him, because, as a few of them said at the time, he was such a good man 'on finance'. He undoubtedly was, having started his business with a partner in the front room of a small house. This was destroyed by fire, but out of the ashes he built a business empire. I had just over five hundred votes and he over two thousand. At the end of the count I refused to shake hands with him, such was my puritanical outlook, because, as I told him, he was a capitalist and as such an enemy! I stood for the Rhondda Council on a few occasions, and could command a respectable vote but never sufficient to get anywhere near winning. It was during the election campaigns, too, that the police used to show on whose side they were. We were often picked up in the nights when we were out chalking slogans, taken into the police station and searched, the chalk confiscated before we were roughly turned out. Still, it was an interesting time. There is no street from Trehafod to Mardy that I have not spoken in with the aid of that old ship's bell which was so heavy that only those with strong wrists could swing it. In addition to these activities I attended the meetings of the miners' lodge and was a member of the lodge committee throughout the period, being one of those who took advantage of a Federation dispensation that lodge committees could have among their representatives up to 25 per cent unemployed.

From 1936 onwards there was a major change of scene for me. From the role of what could be described as an unpaid professional revolutionary – unemployment provided the time and opportunity for this kind of full time activity – I was to move into the more confined sphere of the South Wales miners' federation executive to which I had been elected. Not that I had to look over my shoulder in undertaking political activity, but the position carried with it new duties and responsibilities. Although the change narrowed the frontiers within which I was active, it did open new opportunities within the union and for influencing its policy. But whether or not I had been elected to this executive the character of my activities would have undergone a substantial change. We were in the ante-room of world war two, and industry was being stepped up, giving more employment opportunity for those unemployed. It was the beginning of the change from mass unemployment to relatively full employment, a tragic commentary on our social system, that it took a world war to do it.

The period from 1930 to 1937 had been a very difficult and bitter one for our generation. One might literally describe it as a period of 'riotous living' for the unemployed, without, however, wine, women and song. It was a period when, among those who did battle together, deep and lasting friendships were forged; friendships that had been tested in adversity and had stood the test, based as they were on trust and respect for courage and integrity. There are those who have left the Communist Party and find reason to malign it. I can only state that I was privileged during these turbulent years to have worked and fought in the company of great men, great men not in the positions they held, although they possessed abilities that would have yielded high office had they sought it, but in their dedication to a cause. Of these men I mention only a few who earned and deserved the respect of all who knew them. There was Jack Jones, Clydach Vale, a tower of strength who volunteered and joined the International Brigade at the age of thirtynine, was a prisoner of war there and returned to South Wales to become a very able miners' agent for the Rhondda; Harry Dobson, unassuming and always dependable, with whom I worked closely in the Rhondda and who was killed in action in Spain; Lewis Jones, novelist, orator and leader of many marches, who died suddenly in 1938 after a gruelling day of campaigning for aid for Spain; Len Jefferies, with whom I shared a starvation diet and responsibility during those months when I was deputizing for the communist organizer. These and many others like them were men with whom it would always be safe to go 'lion hunting'. I acknowledge my debt to them and can only hope that some of their strength rubbed off on me.

There is an obvious question to be answered: Was the strife and sacrifice worth while and did it get results? In the short term, the results were not great. The administration of the means test was liberalized, as was the application of the regulations by the assistance boards. In addition, the cuts were restored and a move made to bring new industry and work schemes into the region. It is in the long term that I claim the big advances were made for South Wales. I am certain that the battles we fought on the streets there created a conviction that mass unemployment was a social condition to be avoided at all costs in the future; revolutionary ferment would find the ground all too fertile. Governments now accept that steps must be taken to distribute industry and to build up employment opportunity in what are called development areas. Inducements are offered for firms to settle in those areas and capital investment policy within the country is weighted to take account of areas of relatively heavy unemployment. This applies to all parts of the country and it would indeed be a desperate government that allowed massive unemployment to recur.

More important perhaps, is the fact as history records, that a united front of all labour and progressive organizations compelled a recognition of these grave social problems and the application of policies to deal with them. In short, the unity of working people in pursuit of a common objective can change government policy. It seems irrefutable that a unity capable of bringing about this kind of change can also change governments and social systems when such aims are striven for.

Chapter 8
The Death of Company Unionism

As I have stated earlier, the mining industry was the scene of my interest and activity and especially so from the middle of 1936 when I was elected to the executive committee of the SWMF until my retirement in 1968 as national secretary. It has often been said of me that I was a miner and trade unionist first and a communist second. Judging this in retrospect, I have to admit that it has a great deal of truth in it which became more apparent as my duties and responsibilities within the union increased. It was true, too, of Arthur Horner and of most leaders who have lived and worked in the mining valleys of South Wales. Politics take second place to the trade union job, and if and when they conflict, as they did on occasions for Horner and myself, loyalty to the trade union and its decisions came first. This in my opinion is the only way a communist union official can function and earn the respect of union members and be accepted by supporters and opponents as a person of integrity and principle. I think the process of development is from thinking and acting purely as a communist, to thinking and acting as a communist who has accepted that his primary obligation is to the interest of the union and its members. There are occasions when these two positions do not coincide and where, rightly or wrongly one has to make a judgment and stand by it and face criticism from one's friends, but the point is that the communist with these responsibilities will think and react to situations in a somewhat different way from the communist without which can result in opposing stands being taken in given situations.

This seems particularly to be the case with communists and

109

militants in the mining valleys of South Wales. The South Wales Miners' Federation – the 'Fed' as it was called and is still called in many places – was unique among unions, even among those federated to the Miners' Federation of Great Britain. The Fed was a lot more than a trade union; it was a social institution providing through its local leaders an all-round service of advice and assistance to the mining community on most of the problems that could arise between the cradle and the grave. Its function became a combination of economic, social and political leadership in these single industry communities. After all, these communities existed in narrow valley concentrations, were dependant upon a pit for their existence, and were tightly bound together by this common interest. The leaders of the local miners' lodges were very much more than representatives dealing with problems of wages and conditions of employment in the mines. They were acknowledged social leaders called upon to help and advise in all kinds of domestic and social problems; they were indeed the village elders to whom the people went when in any kind of trouble. I can, in a limited way, testify to the truth of this from my own experience as a miners' agent in the Rhymney valley from 1939 and through the war years. The trade union job dealt with pit disputes, the revision of piecework contracts and compensation claims for injury and disease; in short, it dealt with the many problems arising out of and in the course of employment in the pits. But the job by tradition entailed much more than this. I was a sort of professional letter-writer especially in the village where I lived. Harassed wives who had fallen behind in hire-purchase instalments on some household goods, or had accumulated arrears of rent or any other kind of debt, would require letters to be sent appealing for a stay of action by the firms involved. Many times have I appeared in the local court to testify as to the character of the man or child who had fallen foul of the law and to appeal for leniency, on one such occasion at the assize court in Newport.

It was accepted by the union official and the public that he was obliged to give this service if he could. The Fed was a social institution and acted as such without question. Without doubt, its strength and ties with the communities were based on its intimate involvement in social and domestic affairs. It is a regretable fact that these intimate ties are now withering away and this singular character of the Fed is disappearing and being replaced by a more formal and remote trade union function. The miners' federation lodges were pillars of the communities because the miners' institutes and welfare halls provided places for the social and cultural activity, and their domination of the local labour parties decisively influenced local politics. It is not surprising, therefore, that this kind of background produces a loyalty to the union so strong and primary that the union is regarded as a substitute for a political organization. The Fed, now integrated into the National Union of Mineworkers, still sees itself in many situations as giving political leadership and initiating general political campaigns.

In 1936, the federation was waging a bitter campaign against the South Wales industrial union which had been in progress for a year or more. It was concentrated on the Bedwas and Taff Merthyr collieries, although there were a few other pits where fragments of the organization operated, and a team of federation men were permanently leading the campaign at both places. I was sent in to join the two at Taff Merthyr, Alf Davies, who was later to become president in South Wales following Arthur Horner, and Jack Davies, later to become a miner's agent for Rhondda. They were both very experienced in this kind of campaigning. Jack Davies had been one of those sent in by the MFGB some years earlier in the fight against the Spencer breakaway union in Nottinghamshire and had been sent to prison there; Alf Davies, who was secretary of the Ocean colliery lodges, covering some of the pits where this 'scab' union operated. Every day we were holding meetings, distributing leaflets, arranging interviews if we could manage it with members of the other union, and generally trying to win over these men to the federation. The same kind of effort was being made at Bedwas. In previous months, more direct and forceful measures had resulted in a number of those working for the federation being gaoled, more examples of the partiality of the Glamorganshire police leadership for the coal owners which had led the federation on more than one occasion to bring in justices of the peace to witness

111

their actions; but this and other kinds of protest had very little effect. Action followed within the pits in the form of 'stay-in strikes' which brought many pits to a standstill.

The problem was concentrated in pits belonging to the Ocean colliery company, although both in Nottinghamshire and South Wales, these break-away unions were recognized and encouraged by the coal owners generally. They were clearly company unions, which could not exist without the patronage of the employers and which in times of strife clearly identified themselves with the employers and against the miners' federation. As this is being written, discussions have just finished in Parliament on a new Industrial Relations Bill and on its effect on trade union organization and operations. It is the philosophy of the Bill that equates the non-unionist with the unionist. The non-unionist is given rights which clearly provoke the question of whether the future will produce a number of spurious company-patronized unions comprising these anti-social elements to divide and weaken trade union organization in industry. In conditions of relatively full employment, many employers will encourage this kind of development aimed at redressing the balance of power between employers and workers on the labour market. Company unionism among seamen and miners, which followed the General Strike and miners' strike of 1926, owed its continued existence in no small way to the protection provided by the 1927 Trade Disputes and Trade Union Act. It outlawed certain types of strikes and made picketing more difficult. The Industrial Relations Bill is designed to do the same.

The idea of company unionism can be attractive to certain types of employees and to those who for one reason or another become dissatisfied with industry-wide unions. White-collar workers in many enterprises have favoured this form of association, apparently believing that their particular interests were better served that way. Salary prospects and promotion, they believed, depended on the goodwill and recommendation of management or the employer, and organization was devised so that it would not militate against such interests. This is a philosophy which regards salary and promotion advances as favours and not as rights, but it is a philosophy which over the last few

112

years is being replaced by an employee-employer relationship in which rights are agreed and defined, and where the employee-company association is being replaced by bona fide trade unions. But it would be wrong to believe that the concept of company unionism has ceased to have force. The danger lies not only in a slowing down of the growth of genuine trade unions among white-collared workers, but in the rise of organization in plants and companies in opposition to the existing unions. Plenty of managements and employers will encourage and sponsor such growth. The experience of South Wales and of Nottingham, however, shows it as a development that sooner or later itself becomes the cause of bitter industrial strife and dislocation. While it may seem attractive to some employers as a tactic to weaken existing unions, it is a tactic that can be very costly in the long term.

The idea behind this form of union organization is really that of the corporate state, where employers' unions and the government are combined in a single organization within each industry, deciding all aspects of the industry's operation, especially wages, salaries and conditions of employment.

Two main methods were used in the federation's campaign to eliminate the 'scab' union. One was to organize as much pressure as possible on the companies and management at the pits involved, by activities around and inside the pits, and the other was to engage in almost continuous discussion with the coal owners' association and the individual companies. This twofold line of attack was aimed at getting agreement to withdraw recognition from this organization at the pits where it had membership and on a coalfield basis. When I was sent in the campaign, which had been in progress for a couple of years, had been very active but had made little effective progress. A very strained and bitter relationship had developed between certain federation officials and the Bedwas colliery company and this undoubtedly an impediment to useful discussions. A change in this position followed a change in the leadership of the federation. Both the president and vice-president, Jim Griffiths and Arthur Jenkins (father of Roy Jenkins, one-time Chancellor of the Exchequer in a Labour government) had been elected to Parliament and Arthur Horner

H

113

was elected president. A strong attempt had been made to permit Jim Griffiths to hold both jobs, and, although the president's job as such was not then full-time, a majority of the executive was against one person holding the two positions. It is my opinion that Arthur Horner was without question the ablest negotiator to come out of the British coalfields, and the atmosphere of the discussions changed when he took them over – especially with the Bedwas company where, in addition, federation members in the pits affected were getting so restive that they staged a wave of stay-in strikes. This evoked a tremendous emotional response from other miners and in the mining communities. Attempts by management to force men out of the pit by stopping the supply of food, or by more brutal methods such as blasting stone dust at the place where the men have assembled, as happened on one occasion during this period, arouses such strong anger that management are really unable to take any effective action to break such strikes.

The longest time I can recollect men staying in the pit in an action of this kind was at the Fernhill colliery, Rhondda, when they stayed down for a fortnight. This was in 1936 and I took it upon myself as an executive member to enquire of the secretary of the lodge whether the executive committee could be of assistance. I was told that assistance was not required but when the men came up the pit the executive committee arranged for the men to be taken to a convalescent home to recover from the effects of their over-long period of self-imposed incarceration.

On more than one occasion I have had to go down into pits to meet men engaging in this form of action. I recall going down the Parc colliery, Treorchy, during this same period to try to get a number of stay-in strikers out of the pit. I was with Jack Davies, a very experienced man, and I will never forget the experience. As we approached the men who were assembled not far from the pit bottom in a place made warm by the return air, we had to proceed through two ventilation doors, and as we opened the last one we could hear them singing. They were having a concert to pass away the time, and as we reached them were singing 'Will you love the violets, when you've lost the rose?' a popular song of the day. It sounded beautiful, the voices harmonizing

114

as one would expect of any Welsh choir. We failed to get them to come out of the pit with us because they wanted certain assurances before doing so. On another occasion much later and after I became president I went down into a pit at the top of the Aberdare valley where a stay-in strike was in progress. After a long discussion with them they agreed to come out but not until after 'stop-tap' that night. They had heard from the deputies inspecting the pit that bets had been laid in the village that they would be out before the public houses closed, for their Saturday night drink. It was thought to be a safe bet, such were the reputations of one or two of the leaders, but it turned out a loser!

In my view this form of strike action is one for use only in exceptional circumstances. It is justifiable if there is a refusal to recognize the trade union, or in some circumstances when a pit closure, due to take place, will inevitably have serious social consequences. For obvious reasons it is not the form of action to be discussed and decided in a mass meeting, since if the employer is forewarned he would stop work at the pit. It is therefore an action to be undertaken by a small group, but its effect is to prevent a much larger group from working. In this sense it is undemocratic and should only be used in rare circumstances of the kind referred to and never as a method of forcing a settlement of questions and disputes capable of settlement by other means.

Both the Bedwas and Taff Merthyr problems of union recognition were settled in 1937 by discussion and agreement, Arthur Horner agreeing to represent the union in dealing with the disputes at the Bedwas colliery. The menace of company unionism was stamped out but the strife it caused within communities lasted for many years.

The late 1930s was a period of recovery for the trade union movement in Britain. In South Wales we were involved in big efforts of union recruitment, and in improving mining agreements. Months of negotiation at the end of 1936 and into 1937 resulted in a new coalfield agreement based on one rate for the job throughout the coalfield and involving an increase in wages. It was, in fact, a coalfield wages structure that became the forerunner of a similar *national* agreement between the union and

115

the coal board in 1955. I was a member of the negotiating committee, although Arthur Horner was responsible for negotiating on behalf of the federation. This new agreement applied from April 1937 and I missed the actual launching of it as well as the settlements at Bedwas and Taff Merthyr, having left for Spain.

From the great unemployment battles of 1935 and 1936 up to the outbreak of war in 1939, the political scene was undergoing change. It was the period of a popular front movement in France and of a movement in Britain based on a similar attempt at unity. Early in 1937, the Communist Party, Socialist League and the Independent Labour Party joined forces to campaign on a broad programme of action and against 'fascism, reaction and war'. This brought together the leading personalities of each organization to speak on the same platforms and so Stafford Cripps and Harry Pollitt toured the country aided by James Maxton of the ILP, John Strachey, Aneurin Bevan, and many others. It was a period of political revival created by this movement of left-wing unity. A case could be made out now for a new political revival based on a similar unity of the forces of the left, for the need certainly exists.

At that time mining Members of Parliament were 'responsible' to coalfield unions and not to the national organization. Nye Bevan's part in these united front activities was constantly involving him in trouble with the Labour Party, which threatened him with exclusion and sometimes expulsion. Because of this, the executive committee of the South Wales Miners' Federation arranged a meeting with the miners' MPs on a Saturday morning to consider the complaints against Aneurin. The meetings were always well attended by the MPs, most of whom would be critical of Bevan, and would be carrying the torch for the national executive of the Party. These were really exciting meetings, with men like Jim Griffiths, Dai Grenfell and Ted Williams leading the attack, and Bevan skilfully conducting his own defence. It was excellent training for a man coming into the leading councils of the movement relatively young and raw, as I was. With Horner in the chair and the rest of us adding our voices in support of Bevan, these meetings always ended with the executive committee supporting the position taken by him. He, of course, was

116

confident that this would always happen, the composition of the executive being what it was. We all had a great admiration for Bevan, especially for his skill with the spoken word. I used to sit next to a miners' agent named Sid Jones who had known Aneurin intimately over many years and was himself a well-read man, so that when Nye used apt quotations at these meetings, Sid Jones could identify their author and their source. He once told me that when Aneurin was at the Labour College in Earls Court, London, he was not regarded by the tutors as a very energetic or diligent textbook student, but was brilliant in discussion and debate. He possessed a remarkable memory and an equally remarkable ability to draw upon it in speeches and discussion. During the 1936 hunger march, we worked very closely with him and while we were in London we spent a day in his company, and excellent company he was, warm and full of good humour. At lunch time he took us to meet some of his friends who were gathered in a Soho restaurant, rather a motley crowd of intellectuals who were obviously ardent supporters of his. For tea he took us to his flat but London was a strange place to me then, and still is, and I have no idea where it was. He had not been married very long then but when we arrived at the flat Jennie Lee was not at home so we were unable to meet her as he had intended.

Although there was always this admiration for Aneurin, there were many communists who had worked closely with him in different campaigns who did not completely trust him and who regarded him as unreliable and erratic. His political judgment was not always sound, and he could be wrong, which sometimes influenced his attitude to situations and questions and conflicted with the policy of the communist party and others of the left in the labour movement. But who has perfect political judgment, incapable of error and whose policies are never later proved wrong? Mine have been many times and I judge Aneurin Bevan, as I hope to be judged myself, by the general contribution he made to the trade union and socialist movement. By this assessment, Aneurin Bevan was a great man who served his people well.

The job of rebuilding the strength of the union was not an easy one. Non-unionism was strong especially in Powell Duffryn

117

pits. This was a huge coal combine spread over a large number of collieries in the centre of the South Wales coalfield. In 1938, as part of the preparation for the drive to root out non-unionism, a number of executive members were given the job of making a special investigation into conditions in these pits. Together with a colleague I was allocated to the Rhymney valley, the place where the Powell Duffryn Company originated and where their methods had been applied over a long period. They were un-questionably an efficient organization on the mining side operating on most modern techniques then available and with high standards of productivity. But their methods of dealing with the miners were ruthless and repressive. They got rid of those who stood up to them and were known to find reasons to justify the sacking of more than one lodge officer, and this at a time when it was not easy to find alternative employment, particularly in the Rhymney valley where they were in control.

Three reports were drawn up for the executive committee covering the pits under their management. The report on the Rhymney valley was prepared by me and in the introduction the position there was summed up in these few sentences:

'In the concentration upon the aim of maximum output for minimum cost, the scientific use of men, machines and time is applied. To men it means increased exploitation, and the other factors are used to this end. Greater sub-division of labour, speed-up and tension of the entire process tends to increase the rate of physical exhaustion alarmingly. The machine is used wherever possible to eliminate the more expensive human machine, or alternatively, to simplify, and at the same time, intensify his labour. Time is studied minutely from the standpoint of eliminating all wastage and of extracting maximum productive effort from both men and machines.'

They were undoubtedly leading the field in South Wales in methods of rationalization and were well in advance of other companies. But wages and conditions for the miners were behind the rest of the coalfield as was the organization of the union. The result of this investigation was a planned series of strikes in selected pits where non-unionists were interviewed and persuaded to pay either the arrears of their contributions or the entrance fee of £1, whichever was the less. The strike was maintained until full membership was gained and with all the effort we were putting into it, this usually took little more than a week.

In the middle of 1939, the two miners' agents in the Rhymney valley were leaving; one, Ness Edwards, had been elected to Parliament for the Caerphilly division, and the other was retiring at over seventy years old. The Communist Party discussed whether a communist should be nominated for one of the vacancies, for there were few communists in the valley itself and were not very well-known except in their own localities. My name was put forward as a possible candidate, a suggestion to which I was totally opposed. I was an executive member for the Rhondda and had no desire to move into any other area, a view also strongly held by my wife, a Rhondda girl and an active communist there. However, we were assured that there was no chance whatever of a communist winning and in any case it would be difficult to get nominations. The idea was to take a campaign into the valley to enliven things generally in the union and the pits and to try to build party branches there. I was considered suitable because I had a better knowledge than most of mining conditions there, through the investigation in which I had taken part I agreed that if nominations could be obtained I would stand in the election. Two nominations were obtained, one from the Senghenydd unemployed branch and the other from the Windsor lodge, both situated in the same isolated locality of Abertridwr. It was arranged that I would go in to speak from a car rigged up with a loudspeaker and this I did. I was able to speak as one who had made a critical examination of the conditions under which they worked, and the surprising and totally unwanted outcome as far as I was concerned – and of many of the lodge leaders in in the valley as it later turned out – was that I was elected by the ballot of the members! The executive member of the area was elected first and I came second. I started the job in August 1939, just a month before the war broke out, a miners' agent dealing with disputes for the pits at the upper end of the valley and with compensation claims for the whole of the valley. I had very little experience then of negotiating and practically no knowledge

119

whatever of the law affecting compensation claims. I was in at the deep end again, starting off in a new job with a considerable handicap of inexperience and having to build up relationships with lodge officers, of whom twenty or more had been candidates for the job and whom I had defeated. I am sure that had there been fewer candidates I could not have won, and one other aspect of the election which needs emphasis is that my political beliefs and connections were not hidden, the leaflet which was widely distributed in support of my candidature clearly proclaiming that I was a communist.

During the years that followed, I was preoccupied with the problems of the men in the pits in the area I had been elected to serve. Union organization was weak in many of the pits, earnings compared unfavourably with those of other parts of the coalfield, especially when related to the performance of excessively difficult tasks. However, it was not until the war ended that, by enlisting the aid of the executive committee of the union, we finally succeeded in bringing tasks and earnings in these pits nearer to those operating elsewhere. The pace of work at the coalface was so intense that at around the age of fortyfive men ceased to be able to keep up the pace and opted for other work. Conditions on the face were extremely dusty and pneumoconiosis was increasing fairly rapidly. Men certified as sufferers could not by law continue to work in the pits, and were induced by the insurance company acting for the coal owners to take lump sums in settlement of their claims for weekly compensation. Most of the men affected took up employment in the munitions industry where their earnings were higher than before their illness so that, as the law stood, no weekly compensation was payable. In this situation, the small lump sums offered were accepted, although it was known that the disease was progressive and that many of those taking the lump sums could become totally disabled and die, with both the victim and his dependents having to be maintained from state funds.

The initial months of the war, the Communist Party was seriously divided on whether the war was a 'just' or an 'unjust' one. The fascist forces were entrenched behind their Seigfried Line and the allies behind their Maginot Line. It was undoubtedly a 'phoney' period with much behind-the-scenes political activity aimed at changing the direction of the fascist assault, towards the Soviet Union. The support of the Communist Party depended on whether the party considered it was just another imperialist war or a war against fascism. At first, the party supported it, then reversed to opposition following discussions in Moscow; later when Russia was attacked, the policy reverted to one of support. It seems obvious now that the party gave too much weight to the assessment of the Russian party leaders, a disposition that unfortunately did not end with that experience. However, this is a judgment based on hindsight.

At the time I was too concerned with personal problems to become deeply involved in the controversy. My first wife was carrying our first child as we thought, until the actual birth in May 1940 when identical twins were born. Within a couple of hours of their birth, my wife died. Political controversy for me faded into insignificance against this sudden domestic calamity. But life must go on and I now had the responsibility of caring for twin sons. There were many offers of adoption from friends, but I decided against this.

In 1941 I moved house from the lower to the upper end of the Rhymney valley, living there until I was elected president of the South Wales miners in 1951. On the whole, these were happy years. I was living intimately among my own kind of people, accepted by them as part of the village family.

It was while living in the upper end of the valley, in the little mining village of Pontlottyn, that I met and married the wife who has suffered me for the past twentyeight years. I first met her when dealing with a compensation claim arising from a fatal pit accident to the uncle who reared her, but it was not until some years later that we met again and married in 1943. To Betty must go the credit for having reared our family and of being a devoted mother to seven lusty sons. The wives of trade union leaders are often humorously referred to as 'trade union widows'. There is a good deal of truth in it since they take pretty well the whole burden of caring for the family during the frequent and often long absences of their trade union husbands. Before the first twins reached their fifth birthday, we had added

121

three more sons to the family. Five boys under five years old
was certainly a handful and although we decided to call it a
day with a brood of this size, two further additions arrived after
two intervals of about seven years, and again, sons; not a good
example of family planning maybe, but fortunately a healthy
rugby-playing, sports-loving progeny, comprising a closely knit
and happy family.

Two incidents occurred during my service in the Rhymney
valley which had links with my past activities. One was when I
was required to attend an inquest on a miner who had been
fatally injured in a pit accident. The inquest was being held at
the police station in the pit village where he had lived. I arrived
early and the door was opened by the station sergeant whom
I immediately recognized, but who was obviously having some
difficulty in placing me. I introduced myself as the miners' agent
representing the dependents of the dead man. He then queried
me as to whether we had met before. We certainly had, and the
meeting had been a fateful one for me. He was one of the policemen to whom I had been handcuffed on the journey in 1930
from the Porth police court to Cardiff gaol!

The other incident involved blacklegging by girls from Rhymney and Pontlottyn during a Cardiff laundry strike, where the
union involved was demanding recognition by the employers.
When I was approached by the union to help stop the blacklegging, I readily agreed and apart from public meetings, was
mainly involved in picketing the approach to the local railway
station from which these girls were travelling to Cardiff. One of
the girls complained to the police that she had been forcibly
prevented from boarding the train. This was obviously quite possible in a situation where everyone knew everyone else and where
blacklegging was by tradition despised and condemned. As a
result of this complaint, the Superintendent of the Police visited
my home to warn me as a leader of the picketing that the law
had been broken and that serious charges could be made, which
could command fairly long prison sentences. It was alleged that
provisions restricting picketing in the 1927 Trades Union Act
had been breached and we were warned that although no proceedings were being taken against us on this occasion this warning

would be taken into account in the event of any similar occurrence. We were fortunate, I believe, that a county alderman, who was also a member of the county committee responsible for the police force and a local justice of peace and lay preacher, was with us on the picket-line on the morning concerned. It would have been an embarrassment to the police to have had to include such an eminent and respectable member of society in a charge of unlawful or riotous assembly.

The major event in the mining industry during the war years was the great strike wave during 1944. This arose from an award of a tribunal headed by Lord Porter which provided a new national minimum wage for the industry but which was to comprise payments in cash and in kind. This meant that the cash value of concessionary house coal, and free or cheap housing had to be assessed within the new minimum. In South Wales house coal was assessed at 1s 6d a week, so that the cash minimum for the man receiving coal would be that amount less than the man doing the same job who was not entitled to concessionary coal. I was able to get the lodge committees and mass meetings to accept the award and to continue working. In the event, however, and this was the position throughout the country, they went to work on the Monday following the meetings, but other pits were out, with the result that for a whole week the position was one of complete chaos with some men on strike and others working, some men going in and coming out like a concertina. Logically the principle of the minimum wage calculation was sound, but logic has little force in some situations, and this was one such occasion. Although the award was finally accepted, the assessment of payments in kind in its calculation was short-lived.

The immediate post-war position found the nation facing an acute shortage of both coal and miners. Big reforms in wages and conditions were secured and undoubtedly one of the main factors compelling such reforms was the need to hold and attract manpower to the industry. Arthur Horner became the national secretary of the union and was deeply involved with the Labour government in preparing the act of nationalization of the mines which became effective from 1 January 1947. In South Wales, a new president was elected to follow Horner, in the person of

Alf Davies, who, although lacking the brilliance of his predecessor, was a tough negotiator and fighter. But his health was not so good and slowly deteriorated until his death in 1951. For a few of the summers following the end of the war, four of us used to get down to Cornwall for a long weekend, away from politics and the affairs of the union. The foursome of which I was more of a junior member, included Harry Pollitt, Arthur Horner, and Alf Davies, and we used to stay in a pub in Camborne with friends of Pollitt's, spending the weekend eating, drinking and touring the coves along both sides of the peninsular. Harry Pollitt was great company, full of fun and wit, and able not only to relax himself but also the company he happened to be with. They were indeed some of the happiest weekends of my life.

The relationship between the political left and right in the miners' union during the war years and before was characterized by an absence of open conflict. It was Bill Lawther who in 1946 moved the resolution in the Labour Party conference supporting the affiliation of the Communist Party to the Labour Party. This relationship, however, was disrupted following Churchill's cold war speech in Fulton, USA, in 1946, and led to an open breach between Horner and Lawther in 1947 and to a rift in the ranks in the South Wales Coalfield. It had been decided by the national executive committee of the union that Horner should attend a French miners' conference as a fraternal delegate. It so happened that a French miners' strike coincided with the conference where Horner was making his fraternal speech. Lawther repudiated Horner's speech from London and this led to a not very polite exchange between them over the following days. A sub-committee of the union inquired into the affair and issued a report condemning Horner, without having invited him to meet them. It was rather a sordid business altogether, but Horner was most deeply hurt when we had to tell him of our failure to get support for him in South Wales, where he had given so much of his life.

The story behind this incident did not come to light until some years later, and then, according to Horner, from Lawther himself. It appears that an urgent call had been received at the TUC asking its leaders to meet General Marshall in Paris during the miners' strike, and that Lawther was one of those who went over with other representatives of the General Council. Marshall Aid was involved, its promoters making it clear that the leaders of unions in countries receiving the aid were expected to repudiate the strike. I have myself heard Lawther tell this story and talk of how they were picked up by special plane and whisked over without passports or French currency.

Chapter 9

The Post-war Years

In October 1951, I was elected president of the South Wales Area of the National Union of Mineworkers and in the following February moved from Pontlottyn back to Whitchurch, not far from the cottage where I was born. The new house was semi-detached which as a child I had thought of as occupied by the rich, although they were, I suppose, lived in by the better-off middle class who could afford a couple of servant girls who slept in the tiny attic rooms up under the slates. The house was the property of the union and I paid them less than an economic rent. At the time I became president I was also elected to the national executive committee of the union.

During my period of office as president many reforms and innovations were accomplished. I do not claim sole credit for them but I like to think that my work as president facilitated and expedited their introduction. During these years there was good team leadership in the area and when differences arose I always tried to find a basis for unity. No president could have had a more loyal colleague than I had in Dai Dan Evans, who became vice-president and later the general secretary for the area. Among the reforms was the replacement of the old individual pit concessionary coal agreements by a uniform divisional agreement which provided greater equity to supply and entitlement and a pooling of haulage costs. Then there was the agreement whereby the Coal Board subsidized the fares of miners travelling by public transport to and from the pits, and in 1956 the pit agreements for powerloading were replaced by a divisional agreement. As far back as 1952, I was advocating the need for change in the wages arrangements in operation at the coal face and in 1966 when I was secretary this culminated in the National

Power Loading Agreement which abolished piecework and sub-stituted a national day rate.

An important innovation was the introduction of the Annual Miners' Gala. Before the first gala there was uncertainty about the feasibility of getting such large numbers of miners and their families into Cardiff, since long distances were involved, the coal-fields stretching along the coast from Gloucester to Carmarthen. But a rehearsal was made possible by a change in unemployment insurance regulations, the withdrawal of Section 62 of the Act creating hardship, particularly on the disabled partial-compensa-tion man. The South Wales miners, ever ready to engage in political campaigns, were actively opposing this government mea-sure, and in the winter of 1952 it was decided to call a coalfield demonstration against this government action and to stage it in Cardiff. This was used to serve two purposes, that of a political demonstration and a test as to whether we could get huge crowds into Cardiff from the mining valleys. The demonstration was a great success and despite the cold was well attended, so with this rehearsal behind us we went forward with plans for the first annual gala which took place in June 1953, since when they have continued and improved both in the range of the support they attract and in their political and cultural content, although once when I was arguing for the inclusion of jazz bands, which were reminiscent of our big strikes, a close friend and colleague forcefully declaimed against them, contending that 'they were not bloody culture'. His point of view won the day then but they have since been included. The whole purpose of a Gala is to bring crowds of people together, to provide entertainment, edu-cation and a day's enjoyment, and in the process to get a political message across. The 'masses', fortunately, are not as puritanical as some of their leaders.

The other annual event introduced when Alf Davies was presi-dent was the Miners' Eisteddfod, now accepted as the best one day eisteddfod in Wales. In 1957, on 5 October and our Eisteddfod Day, we arranged a transatlantic telephonic link-up with Paul Robeson in New York. At that time, this great inter-national artist and champion of the Negro people was virtually a prisoner, his passport having been taken from him and his

127

movements within America being very restricted. We were campaigning for his freedom and the return of his passport. I was privileged to speak to him from our eisteddfod and he in turn spoke and sang to the great audience assembled, an audience tearfully hushed as his great bass voice echoed through the hall as he sang 'All Through the Night'; 'This Little Light of Mine'; 'All Men are Brothers'; and songs so relevant to the occasion. The Treorchy Male Voice Choir sang for him an old Welsh ballad, 'Y Delyn Nur' but the climax came when the great audience and the choir sang with deep feeling, 'We'll Keep a Welcome in the Hillside'. When his passport was returned to him some time later he came to us in South Wales, meeting in person the people who had sung to him across the Atlantic Ocean and who had tried to help in restoring his freedom to travel and sing outside the Americas.

In this very brief appraisal of union activity it would be unforgiveable not to pay tribute to the marvellous work of the doctors and nurses for the service they render to injured miners. Broken bones and lacerated bodies are part of the price paid by miners in the getting of coal, and although safety standards are constantly improving, accidents are all too frequent. We owe much to the doctors and nurses in the local hospitals for their efforts in repairing this human damage. But the greatest work of all is done in the rehabilitation centres. In South Wales this centre was famous not only for the excellent service of the remedial staff and visiting surgeons in uniting broken bones and rebuilding men to their former abilities but, infinitely more, for the two characters in charge. The Matron and Sister of the Talygarn Rehabilitation Centre in South Wales were revered by the miners of the coalfield and by the union leaders. No combination of two people could have been more eminently suitable for undertaking the responsibilities and no two people could have discharged them better. Now in well-earned retirement, Margaret Irwin and Connie Thomas, still remembered by miners as Matron and Sister, are among the great names of those who have served with distinction the miners of South Wales.

Although the accident rate in the pits is steadily being reduced and the big disasters less frequent, the dread of tragedy is an ever present condition in mining homes and communities. I can recall two explosions during my years as president in South Wales. Together with the Chairman of the Divisional Coal Board, Mr D. M. Rees, I went along to the South Pit, Glyncorrwyg, immediately we heard of the disaster there. Although the casualties were light compared with those in disasters like Senghenydd and Gresford, where the death toll was in hundreds, the grief of the stricken community was no less. Looking down into the top of the deep, narrow Afon valley from the top of the surrounding hills, seeming always to be enveloped in cloud, the pit and the community built around it presented a grim picture. At the pit head the village people stood silent, expressing a grief and anxiety that could be felt. In the colliery office the pit and union leaders were doing everything possible to organize the rescue activities but there was little we could do except to give sympathy and support. The subsequent investigation showed that the explosive mixture formed by the accumulation of gas and air had been ignited by a sufficiently hot spark splintered off from a rusty hammer striking a metal roof support. The roof support was made of a metal alloy containing magnesium, and the explosion was later reproduced in the laboratories of the mining scientists using the same combination of elements. The metal roof supports were immediately withdrawn from use throughout the industry.

The other explosion was on 22 November 1956 at the Lewis Merthyr Colliery, Porth, the pit next down the valley from the one in which I had worked. The source of ignition here was considered to have been caused by a collision of two pieces of rock, probably iron-stone, falling from a cavity in the roof. A number of men, including the colliery manager, had been badly burned and we visited them at the special treatment hospital for burns and skin grafting at Chepstow. The condition of these men is hard to describe; their hands and faces were badly swollen and had the appearance of having been fried. They were quite cheerful when we met them, and to our inexperienced eyes seemed certain to survive their injuries. Nevertheless, they died within a week or so. My paramount feeling in such situations is one of helplessness, of realizing a lethal hazard too late. As a colleague

I

of mine puts it, disaster is the father of reform in mining safety regulations.

But the pit takes its toll in death from communities too. I visited the scene of the awful Aberfan disaster the day after it happened. The tip moved down on the school and houses on Friday morning, 21 October 1966, and I was there on the Saturday with the union safety engineer, Keith Saunders. In borrowed knee-high wellington boots we trudged in the pouring rain through tip sludge and slurry feet deep. Most of the bodies had then been recovered, both those of the children who had been trapped in the school and of the people who had been buried alive in their homes. There was no lack of assistance, for scores of men, drenched to the skin, were still carrying on the search for bodies. As soon as we arrived at the colliery and met the local union leaders, we were told that the tip which had caused the calamity had been started over a spring and stream that the local people, during the 1926 lock-out, had damned up for the children to bathe in. There is hardly a valley in South Wales without at least one pit-heap overhanging the side of the mountain, where the original planners had used the sloping side of the hill to assist in the disposal of the pit's waste product. I travelled every day for about ten years along a road in the Rhymney valley past one such tip, called Spion Cop by the local people, which overhung the village of Brithdir. Many times had I passed the tips at Aberfan, poised as they were on the mountain slope behind the village. We frequently condemned these heaps as monstrous eyesores, but we failed to realize their potential danger. Although we can plead that we are not specialists in such matters, I believe that union leaders must accept some responsibility for the failure to anticipate and take action to avert this terrible disaster. One of my elder sons is employed by the firm now engaged in moving the whole series of these tips to the flat surface of the mountain and was himself employed on the site during the early months of the operation.

I referred earlier to my first presidential address in 1952. In the same speech I drew attention to a development which faced the union then and has continued to do so throughout the years, the problem of unofficial strikes. My views on the subject now are much the same as they were then:

'I cannot recall a time during which there has been such internal upset in the union as in the latter half of the period since the last annual conference. This has been dealt with in a recent special conference. I mention it again only to underline the paramount need to maintain maximum unity in our ranks. The leadership of the union is the area executive committee elected biennially by ballot vote of the members. It is an executive committee of working miners, not full-time officials. No lodge or group of lodges must be allowed to usurp its authority and leadership. This is an industrial organization comprising many political outlooks. Every political outlook can be freely expressed either in meetings or conferences called to discuss questions of policy. But once decisions have been reached they must be accepted and applied by all. The right of the minority to seek to change policy is not challenged provided the change is sought by constitutional methods. Our strength in gaining redress to grievances whether industrial or political is represented in our organizational unity, in the progressive character of our policy, in the loyalty and support of the lodges and members for such a policy. If we all keep faith with these basic considerations we can move forward together unhindered by internal friction.'

There were two aspects to this unofficial movement; one was the sectional character of pit strikes, the other the calling of unofficial conferences of lodges by unofficial leaders to decide action on issues often already being dealt with by the union. The position became so serious that in the annual conference and special conference I had to attack those responsible, both communist and labour militants. In the 1956 conference I described the situation thus:

'The sequel to this kind of irresponsible conduct is "tit-for-tat" strikes that have occurred all too often in the last twelve months. Usually such actions are initiated by pieceworkers, and in certain pits have become so serious that any semblance

131

of unity within the lodge has been completely destroyed. Elected leadership is ignored – as are the interests of the general body of workmen; union organization and policy count for nothing, the selfish interests of the few being regarded as paramount.'

The point stressed all the time was that the union existed to redress grievances and should be given the chance to do this before action was resorted to. The problem was not only discussed within the union but inside the Communist Party too. I argued the position not only in South Wales but also in London, with Harry Pollitt and other leaders coming to South Wales for discussions with us. I argued that the union in South Wales was a militant organization and that unorganized movement and leadership among miners outside the union was destructive and not constructive. The Communist Party at that time accepted this reasoning and did what it could to reduce this kind of internal conflict which dissapated unity and strength. It would seem, however, that what was accepted then has since been abandoned, to judge by the events that took place in that coalfield during 1970.

The contrast between the problems of the interwar years and those of the post-war period is very marked, with the employment position as the greatest single outstanding feature. In the 1920s and 1930s, mass unemployment was heavy and continuous; the 1950s and 1960s were years of relatively full employment, as of course were the war years. The men who led the great fights against unemployment and for the right to work were themselves now in work. My old friends Len Jefferies, Phil Abrahams, Jack Jones and a host of other unemployed leaders were in employment, active in the trade unions, trades councils and local government. In Liverpool, Leo McGree was working at his trade before becoming a full-time officer for the Amalgamated Society of Woodworkers, while Finlay Hart was back at his trade too, and holding a leading position both on the Clyde and nationally in the boilermakers' union. With the change of scene came a change in the problems which confronted my generation, problems which for the succeeding generation conditioned their entry into the industrial, social and political life of the nation. As was the case follow-

ing the first world war, the reconstruction boom was short-lived
and the country was again facing serious economic and financial
problems. The trade union and labour movement was intensely
agitated by wage restraints, attacks on the welfare state, hydrogen
bomb tests and limited wars – a rich miscellany of industrial,
social and political issues performing the initiation rites for post-
war youth.

In the mining industry after a decade of relative prosperity
when coal was king in the energy empire, a period when the
union was preoccupied with lifting the status of its members and
when reforms and improvements could be paid for by an increase in the price of coal, the scene changed back again to one
we were more accustomed to, a crisis of over-production. Energy
supplies were in excess of demand and the energy industry
selected to take the full effect of the crisis and subsequent cut-
back of production was the one indigenous to Britain, coal. The
oil industry, once a complementary source of fuel to coal, became its main competitor with fuel oil. Later the competition
against coal was to be intensified with the development of nuclear
power stations for the generation of electricity and the discovery
of North Sea gas. The rapid contraction of the mining industry
provided the economic and political climate of my whole period
as secretary for the National Union of Mineworkers. It was the
beginning of a programme of pit closures and manpower run-
down that in a decade halved the size of the industry and the
number of pits and men employed, leaving mining villages
derelict.

I was still president in the South Wales coalfield at the start
of the pit closures to cut back production. In fact I was leading a
miners' delegation from South Wales in the Soviet Union when
the Divisional Coal Board announced that seven South Wales pits
were to close simultaneously. We had been visiting pits and new
mining towns in the Donoass coalfield of the Ukraine and were
about to be taken to Sochi on the Black Sea for a holiday and
rest. I had to abandon the holiday and return to South Wales
to deal with the situation the announcement had created. We
produced a pamphlet in which we set out the effects of these
closures in terms of unemployment and hardship for men and

133

communities. It meant that over half the men displaced would immediately become unemployed, and as the pits selected were the sole means of employment for isolated villages these villages would become derelict. In the receiving pits, men in the older age groups were being pressed to retire to make way for younger men. We argued that the Coal Board's appraisal of the situation was too narrow and ignored fundamental facts. We presented four main arguments which were as appropriate then for South Wales as they were to become for the rest of the country in the following years.

Summarized, these arguments were, first, that the government was pursuing economic and financial policies which slowed down economic growth; that in such a stagnant economy competition from other fuels was intensified but the closure of pits now could cause a shortage of fuel with the growth of the economy; that in socialist countries all sources of fuel were expanded, and that in the context of world needs there was a chronic scarcity of all forms of energy. Although this fourth point stresses the need for increasing energy supplies, it is also the classic indictment of capitalism and applies equally to all aspects of its operations. The substance of this case we made against these initial closures in South Wales became the policy of the union nationally in its discussions with the Coal Board, and the government in its efforts to reverse their policies.

I moved to my new post in London in April 1959 and my successor in South Wales was Will Whitehead, who had been secretary of the Parc and Dare lodge, the biggest lodge in the coalfield, and later a miners' agent in the Aberdare valley. He was an extremely able man and an excellent negotiator and leader, and I think he would have followed me as national secretary had not a serious illness unfortunately compelled him to retire prematurely from union office. His period as president was a difficult one because South Wales became, with Durham and Scotland, the areas with the heaviest programme of closures, and where the social consequences caused the greatest hardship. During the weeks before the actual closure on the seven pits in the early months of 1959, resistance by strike action was considered, but when we tested the coalfield on this through a delegate conference the reaction was against it, understandably, because there were many uneconomic pits whose miners feared that action of that kind could precipitate their own closure. This was a constant factor throughout the whole period. The tactic of a stay-in strike was also considered and was discussed seriously at one of the pits facing closure but as the pit itself was cold and damp no action was taken. The protest movement against closures had to assume other forms both during the short experience I had of them in South Wales and throughout Will Whitehead's presidency. In protest against the first seven closures we organized a representative demonstration to London to support a meeting we had arranged with the Minister of Power, Lord Mills, and to lobby the members of Parliament. Unfortunately a widespread fog delayed the arrival of the bus loads of representatives in London, and although we met the Minister we got no satisfaction from the discussion. We were told to face economic reality, that coal no longer monopolized the energy market, that cheaper fuels were available and that consumers' freedom of choice and not action by the government would determine the size of the coal mining industry. This indeed became the theme song of successive ministers acting for both governments when in power. The struggle to keep the pits open, to stop the run-down of the industry, to save the mining areas from desolation became the principal pre-occupation of the union during my whole period of office as its national secretary and many and varied were the methods we tried in our efforts to accomplish this.

The first major national effort was to organize a study conference which was held in the Grosvenor House Hotel, London, on the last weekend in March 1960, from the Friday to the Sunday. The chairman was Sir Geoffrey Crowther, and among the forty or so people who attended from industry, commerce, and communications were such as Sir Robert Shone, CBE of the Iron and Steel Board, Sir Christopher Hinton, chairman of the Central Electricity Generating Board, Mr C. M. Vignoles, CBE managing director of Shell-Mex and B.P.; Mr G. W. Powell, managing director of Esso Petroleum, and last but not least, the Right Honourable Harold Wilson, MP, OBE. This was a high-powered conference, bringing together men of influence in a world of

135

energy. Three papers were put forward for discussion, dealing not only with coal but with the problem of energy as a whole, stressing the need for planning and the conservation of the production and consumption of primary fuels. As could be expected discussion was good on the points raised in the papers and the conference was a success insofar as it presented the problems of the coal industry and won an appreciation for them. When the representatives of the oil industry explained and defended their position, differences arose, but in relation to subsequent events it was perhaps the speech of Harold Wilson that merits attention, and I quote the summarized version approved by him from the report of the conference. He

'thought there were four reasons for cushioning the fall in coal demand. There was first the problem of social hardship, secondly, it was quite clear we were going to need the industry in the future but it was an industry that it was difficult to reactivate if you let it run down too far, both physically and in terms of manpower. Thirdly, there was a very important balance of payments reason for making full use of our indigenous fuel industry. Fourthly, there was the problem of the strategic vulnerability of our oil supplies, even allowing for diversification.

'It was decisively a Government responsibility not to let the coal industry run down and possibly out. There must be certain priorities. Indigenous fuel must come first, home refined oil second and imported products third. The Government should set the target for coal production for some years ahead. Even if it were decided that the target should be slightly lower each year, there would be some stability, and both the Board and the union would find it much easier to plan their working.

'How could this be done? The Government could not decide how each consumer should plan his fuel requirements. But the Government had it in its power to influence such decisions. They did to every one of us every day through fiscal policy. Harold Wilson favoured the fiscal approach as a means of influencing rather than physically determining the rate of consumption of coal as against oil.

136

'Finally two arguments had been used against any action at all. The first was Mr Vignoles assertion that the oil industry was the biggest invisible earner. Unfortunately, this was a subject on which we never obtained any figures. To support that statement much more information was needed. The other argument was freedom of choice. This was an argument used by the Government. It could lead to disastrous consequences for the coal industry and the country. Moreover, the Government had no hesitation in limiting consumers freedom of choice in respect of a whole range of goods, by fiscal and other means. And would freedom of choice be permitted if it were to result in large imports of Russian oil? The "freedom of choice" argument was at best a shaky one.'

It is not my purpose to denigrate the Labour government for its treatment of the coal-mining industry from 1964 onwards when it came to power. The arguments advanced by Harold Wilson became the arguments we used to Labour ministers of power and to Harold Wilson himself, when Prime Minister, but with singularly little effect.

The Home Policy Committee of the Labour Party, in May 1964 in a letter to the union, following our joint discussions, promised the coal industry a minimum production target of 200 million tons a year which would increase as the economy expanded. A few months after the Labour Party came to power, Sid Ford, who succeeded Ernest Jones as president, and I were invited to meet George Brown, then responsible for economic planning and whose signature was on the letter we had received from the Home Policy Committee. That morning he had the distasteful job of informing us that not only was the 200 million tons definitely not on, but that production from the coal industry would be cut back. The cut-back envisaged was set out in the Coal Plan of September 1965, which acknowledged a cut-back over the eight years up to 1964 of 30 million tons to 193 million tons and estimated that by 1970 this would decline to a range of between 170 and 180 million tons, a pretty wide margin even for this kind of guessing game. In the same period, it was estimated that manpower would fall by about 179,000 to

137

480,000. How much of a guessing game it was is exemplified by the facts. Results for the financial year 1969–70, calculated on 28 March 1970, show production from deep mines and opencast to be down to a little more than 147 million tons, with manpower down to a little more than 305,000 men on books, which means an effective labour force of much less. Against this, consumption was 162,756,000 tons, or fifteen million tons in excess of production!

It is true, of course, that with the National Plan came legislation to write off around £400 million of the industry's capital liabilities, with new provisions for payment for men made redundant, as well as the ban on imported coal and the continuation of the fuel oil tax applied by Selwyn Lloyd when he was Conservative Chancellor. But these measures did nothing to remedy the real problem. The rapidity of the run down had destroyed confidence in the future of the industry and the younger men were leaving for more secure employment. Pits were closed to redistribute the available labour to the most profitable pits. Time and time again we warned ministers and the Prime Minister that the day would come when they would need the pits and the men and they would be short of both, as happened in 1940 when they closed pits following the fall of France. This is the position now, with the demand for coal exceeding supply, so that coal is again being imported. Basically the policy of the Labour and Conservative governments differ very little. Both use 'consumers' freedom of choice' arguments, too, and when reminded of Harold Wilson's statement to the study conference, reply that new factors requiring new approaches have entered the situation, the new factors being nuclear power stations, promoted by them on a big scale. Jointly with the Coal Board, we pressed the need for alternative industry and finance for the Board to set up light industry in goods for use in the pits to provide light employment for the disabled men who were being discarded. The Prime Minister promised that research would be carried out on the aspect of social hardship, costing the payments made directly and indirectly to redundant men and the steps taken by the government to attract new industry, against the cost involved in keeping open certain pits where social consequences were par-

138

ticularly harsh. We were promised, too, a further research on the comparative costs of nuclear power production, taking all factors into account, and that this would be done before the Seaton Carew station was authorized. This demand was pressed following the Coal Board statement that the real and full costs of nuclear power production were not being revealed, and that electricity from this source was more costly than from coal. We did not see the sums and were told only what we had heard before, that they favoured nuclear power.

One of the last discussions on this problem in which I took part and at which the then Prime Minister, Harold Wilson, was present, was on the eve of the Labour Party Conference at Scarborough in 1967. It was at this meeting that the Prime Minister announced the government's intention to instruct the Coal Board to suspend pit closures for the winter period and that they would meet any losses incurred by this postponement. Unemployment was then heavy and rising and was expected to be particularly serious as the winter developed. The government was worried at this prospect and obviously to allow these closures (some sixteen or seventeen pits were in the pipeline) was bound to create unemployment. It was really a nice bit of political window-dressing for the conference the following week and showed that the government was worried about the opposition in the labour and trade union movement to the rising unemployment. At the meeting, I put the main case for the union, comparing the announcement to postpone closures with the position of the man condemned to hang, who, on the evening of the day fixed for the hanging, was told by the prison governor that his hanging had been postponed because the hangman was sick. He was still to hang, just as the pits in the pipeline would still close, only the closures would be concentrated into a shorter period and would thus avoid swelling the unemployment figures at a time embarrassing to the government.

On this same theme, I must mention what was for me a most thrilling moment in my life. In November 1967, the national union called for a big demonstration meeting in the Central Hall, London. A new government statement on fuel policy issued earlier in the month assessed the effect of the discovery and extraction

139

of North Sea gas on the fuel economy of the country. The coal estimates forecast in the 1965 National Plan were drastically revised. Coal consumption for 1975 was estimated at 120 millions, including two million tons of exports. The Coal Board estimated that only 160,000 men would be required in the industry to produce that amount of coal which would, of course, aggravate the already serious fall in job opportunity, especially in those areas and communities entirely dependent upon the coal industry to provide employment. The coal industry has been bedevilled from the middle 1950s with spurious estimates. In 1955–56 we were told there would be a market for 240 million tons; later it was to be 200 million tons but with the prospect of this increasing; in 1965 it was 170 to 180 million tons for 1970. Investment in the industry is related to the expectation of markets four or five years ahead because, in an extraction industry operating below ground and contending with the forces of nature, the returns on capital investment are not realized for several years. Millions of pounds have undoubtedly been wasted in planning for a production capacity that in the event has not been required, adding seriously to the heavy financial burdens of the industry. The history of disastrous estimating by the experts has landed this nation in its present predicament of a serious and continuing fuel shortage, no matter how short-lived it may be. It will take a few more years into the 1970s to make good the shortage of smokeless fuel and coking coal, although I have no doubt that in time this will happen. However, it need never have occurred.

When the Labour government's new fuel policy statement was about to be debated in the House of Commons, we held our November demonstration meeting to mobilize all the support we could for the opposition inside the Parliamentary Labour Party. All Labour members with pits in their constituencies were invited and it was estimated that some seventy to eighty actually turned up, together with over three thousand union representatives from all the coalfields of the country with union officers and executive members in attendance and with the press well represented. Earlier in the day we had, as national officers, met the Minister of Power to protest against this accelerated run down of the industry and were to report on it to the conference. On the platform were Ford, the president of the union and who reported the meeting with the minister, Jennie Lee, chairman of the Labour Party, Victor Feather and myself, all of whom were scheduled to speak. It is difficult to describe the atmosphere of this meeting. The Central Hall was packed and an overflow meeting had gathered in the lesser hall to which the speeches were relayed. The report on the meeting with the minister gave the audience no grounds for optimism about future prospects; Jennie Lee, when she spoke, attracted opposition from some of the Scottish delegates and the meeting was in a critical mood, wanting a more forthright attack on government policy. I had prepared notes for my speech, detesting to read prepared speeches, and my notes were forthright enough could I but use them properly. Just as there are occasions when things go wrong for a speaker, so are there occasions when they go just right, and this was an occasion when they went right for me and, I hope, for the meeting. I challenged every claim of government policy and set out to prove how wasteful and disastrous it would be; how beneficial it would be for private enterprise, especially for the oil monopolies, and how damaging it would be to the nationalized coal industry and to the whole concept of nationalization. I tried to describe how unemployment, idleness and poverty demoralized men so that they accepted standards of conduct and behaviour they would never dream of accepting while in employment. I suppose it was a mixture of politics and human appeal because, before I had quite finished the speech at the end of a forceful denunciation and while I was still on my feet, I received a spontaneous standing ovation. And on that climax I ended, taking the advice of Vic Feather, who was sitting next to me.

The demonstration meeting had a tremendous effect within the Parliamentary Labour Party, and when Ford and I went down to the House one evening a little later and met all the labour members who had been present, we discussed tactics for a party meeting and found that quite a number of members were disposed to vote against the policy both in the party meeting and when the policy came before Parliament. There was a strong

141

sprinkling, too, of those who were anxious to avoid this kind of showdown, and it was this point of view that ultimately carried inside the party and government, because, it seems, the policy statement was not debated in Parliament, but remained, of course, on the records as a statement of government policy.

We were fortunate at this time to have had as chairman of the miners' group of Members of Parliament, an ex-miner Tom Swain, member for North-east Derbyshire. One got the impression that some of his colleagues regarded him with some disfavour because of his aggressive bluntness, but he was unquestionably a powerful champion of the miners' case among other MPs and in Parliament itself. He tackled the job as a pitman would, with an unrefined directness especially aimed at those junior ministers who were of the miners' group but who were taking their stand with the Government and in opposition to the group.

Before the big demonstration meeting, some areas of the union put strong pressure on the national executive committee to give a lead for strike action. Such action would of course be against government policy and in that context would be a 'political strike'; in addition, it would be a strike against a Labour government, not the easiest combination for getting wide support in the labour movement. Nevertheless, it was a tactic to be considered seriously, and at a national executive meeting I submitted a resolution which put up alternatives for consideration, but whose main suggestion which alone seemed practicable to me, was for guerrilla strikes – that is, the selection of certain pits where the cessation of production has an immediate effect upon some important industrial activity like power stations or steel works. I always had reservations about an all-out strike against pit closures, because I considered that certain pits would be closed in the process and miners affected by this would hold the union responsible for their close-down. I was also afraid that the strike might not be one hundred per cent solid because men in the more vulnerable pits would have this same fear. However, the main problem of the guerrilla strike was that the pits selected would be those where the threat of closure was most remote and where the miners themselves were not directly involved, so that the sacrifice – even with strike pay – would fall upon those who

142

were not themselves faced with the prospect of closure. Of course, difficulties arise from any form of direct action but it is as well to try to anticipate them. However, the national executive committee did not favour any form of direct action and decided to carry on with the methods and public campaigning as before, a policy which when put to a special delegate conference in the spring of 1968 was carried by a very big vote.

As national secretary of the union, I used to speak at miners' gala meetings, occasionally with the Prime Minister and other government leaders on the platform, but always at the Durham Big Meeting where the national secretary was a guest speaker by 'standing order' and the leader of the Labour Party was always invited to speak. The Prime Minister was present at my last speech to the Big Meeting on 20 July 1968 and I took advantage of this to tell him and the meeting how blatantly inaccurate were the government estimates in the 1967 fuel policy statement. The Prime Minister had told us when we met him in the previous March that if the manpower figures on which the White Paper had been based were incorrect, the government would of course look at the matter again. My comment at the Big Meeting, after quoting this, was that we had had a bellyful of reviews already and that after each previous one the coal industry's difficulties had been intensified. It is a desperately frustrating exercise to try to change the views of a government by argument and pleading, which is the main reason, I have no doubt, why unions and workpeople from time to time use their ultimate sanction of withdrawing labour in the belief that actions speak louder than words.

Two main arguments are used by those who support the contraction of the coal industry. Coal, they say, has no place in the developing, new, scientific and technological age; it belongs to the past. My answer is that the sources of energy so far discovered are in the earth's crust and in limited quantities, and that it is a betrayal of the interests of future generations for this generation to waste and sterilize these limited resources. A further reply is that the two most advanced industrial countries of the world, America and Soviet Russia, both with far greater alternative fuel resources than Britain, coal production is being in-

143

creased. Another argument used by those who favour the contraction is that mining is such a dirty and dangerous occupation that the sooner it is closed down the better, and that the Miners' Union opposes the contraction of the industry because it is emotionally involved. It is, of course, true that mining is a difficult industry but so is deep sea fishing, and so is the mining of uranium, the base mineral for nuclear power. In fact, the longterm hazards of nuclear power production will not be known for years, but no-one can deny that the health of workers is at risk, as is all living matter, in this development. That we are emotionally involved is not denied, but it is an emotion born of a knowledge of the social havoc caused by the rapid contraction. I answered this kind of criticism in an article published early in November 1967, and to quote from it seems an appropriate way to end this story of the post-war problems of the mining industry and my involvement in them :

'Of course we have a vested interest and are emotionally involved. It is an interest and involvement with people and communities. I took a leading part in three hunger marches from South Wales against the dereliction and misery forced upon mining communities in the 1930s. In 1936 over five hundred of us marched from South Wales, joining thousands from all over the country, and supported by the entire Labour and Trade Union movement. We were fighting for economic security, for jobs, against forced migration, and for the preservation of our homes and our homeland. It would be a shocking betrayal of that struggle not to fiercely resist a similar threat today. The stark reality is that induced decay of coalmining means the social death of many mining communities. I wonder sometimes if those who decide policies to precipitate the contraction of the coal industry have any idea as to what a pit closure means to the community built around it. It is the death of a creation that gave the community life and sustained that life no matter how deprived and anguished it might have sometimes been. Closure thus represents a disaster as poignant and harrowing as a death in the family. For older people it creates a sense of helplessness and hopelessness. No fancy

144

clichés of "national interest", "redeployment" and "mobility of labour" or of "increased dole payments" by the economists, the politicians or the technocrats can rationalize out of existence these very real feelings.

'The dignity and self-respect of people must be preserved. Economic security must be guaranteed. The miners do not resist change if they are convinced that it is necessary. But they will insist that if change there must be, then their folk must not suffer economically or socially. This emotional involvement is probably at its strongest in single industry communities, but I am sure it exists, even if to a lesser extent, in any community of people facing the loss of their traditional source of employment.'

I had a brief membership of the General Council between the 1960 and 1961 Congresses. It can be truthfully stated that I got on it by accident but was put off by design. The history of nominations to the General Council in the records of the miners union is a curious one. Until the miners' conference of 1933 only two nominations were required by the TUC and these were always the chairman and secretary. In 1934, three were nominated; Ebby Edwards, the secretary, Joseph Jones, the president, and Will Lawther, the vice-president. All three were elected at the 1935 Congress. In 1939, Edwards, Lawther and Horner were nominated, and this was the first time the miners' union lost its monopoly of the available seats. A. R. W. Williams was elected, obviously to keep Horner off, and he was secretary of the North Wales quarrymen, with a membership of about eight thousand. He was followed later by R. J. Jones from the same small union, which was a kind of autonomous section of the Transport and General Workers' Union. So, although the miners could nominate three, only two could expect to be elected at Congress. This position continued throughout the secretaryship of Arthur Horner; each year he was one of the three nominees but was never elected. When Lawther retired, the secretary of the Lancashire area, on his first nomination, was chosen in preference to the national secretary of the union.

My first nomination as one of three came in 1959, for the 1960

K

Congress. The president of the Yorkshire area, Alwyn Machen, was another nominee, and was in fact elected by ballot vote to succeed Ernest Jones as president of the national union, but he died before he could take office. This left only two nominees from the miners, Albert Martin and myself. The third nomination was no longer filled by the quarrymen, the place having been taken by a representative of the National Association of Colliery Overmen and Deputies, in the person of their national secretary, Bart Walsh. He died early in 1960 and so the unions in Group I were confronted with a unique situation. Here was the chance for the miners to assert their determination to get three of their own men elected. On the question of who was to replace Walsh the National Executive Committee, on 21 January, decided:

'That no nomination be submitted for the present casual vacancy and that the policy of submitting nominations for the General Council of the TUC be reviewed.'

At this meeting Sam Watson of Durham, a Labour Party leader suggested that the union should decide to nominate only two and thus end this farce. The decision that day meant the acceptance of only two representatives from the miners, and it was illogical to continue to nominate three. But logic has no place in political prejudice and the union returned to its previous position of nominating three. Thus when the 1961 Congress came round Collingridge of Yorkshire, the third nomination was elected and I was deposed. There was supposed to be an unwritten law that once on, the TUC would not put a member off, and certainly more than a few members could only have retained their seats by this rule, but that law, too, had very definite political limitations. I heard also that some NUM leaders, on the eve of the Congress, had made it known that two of their nominees were loyal members of the Labour Party, and that a communist ought not to be given preference over them.

This matter caused some interest at the time and has often been referred to since, hence this rather lengthy explanation of what was involved. Whether a particular individual is on or off the Council is not a world-shattering event, and when questioned about this I have replied, with pardonable immodesty, that their loss was greater than mine. The fact is, however, that my removal was connived at as much by certain leaders in the NUM as by the TUC. The issue was discussed later in an annual conference when the resolution to nominate only two candidates was defeated, the argument against quite clearly indicating the view that if the three were Labour men they would be elected. Three Labour men were put forward in 1964, but only two of them were elected, the TUC operating the unwritten law that they did not depose sitting members provided they belonged to the right political club. As for my own position, I refused further nomination after 1961, not being prepared to be the kind of 'Aunt Sally' that Arthur Horner was during the whole period of his secretary-ship. It was not only in relation to the TUC that the miners' union exercised this political discrimination. The executive committee unanimously nominated me for the vice-presidency of the Miners' International Federation, but it did not stop a leading official of the union canvassing opposition to my nomination among affiliated unions. The president of the International informed me that he and others had been approached but had told the canvasser to do his own dirty work within the union in Britain. However, such incidents were infrequent, the general climate within the union being one of great tolerance for the differences in political outlook and attachment of its leaders.

Nevertheless, that year on the General Council gave me a good insight into its working, and did open up avenues for promoting discussions with representatives of government and industry on general questions and those of special interest for miners. There were difficulties too. This was the year when there was scarcely a meeting of the Council, the position of the Electrical Trades Union figuring large on the agenda. The charges of ballot rigging were obviously of concern to the TUC who finally decided on the expulsion of the union from the TUC. I abstained when the vote was taken, finding it very difficult to join forces with those on the Council whose attitude to the charges was more conditioned by their rabid anti-communist prejudices than by an objective examination of the facts. No one could defend what had happened in this union and I certainly did not try. It was also a year when the question of policy on the hydrogen bomb was the

147

subject of heated argument between leaders of the Labour Party and powerful union leaders within the TUC. All in all, it seems reasonable to accept the conclusion that it was not the best year for a communist trade union leader to be successfully initiated into this select and enclosed circle.

In the early years of my service as national secretary, I prepared a paper for discussion on possible methods of reorganization, aimed at creating one united constituent area organization in each coal board division. I have always accepted the view that union organizational structure in a nationalized industry should be adapted to that of the employers. In this way there should be only one union organization to face the organization of the National Board running the industry, at regional and national level. In the nationalized coal industry, this meant at that time one organization of the union in each Coal Board division. In the case of the Coal Board, this would have meant again having to adapt union structure some years later when the Coal Board divisions were split up into about seventeen areas. The annual conference of 1961 had remitted to the national executive committee resolutions dealing with union organization and the committee had promised that a report would be prepared with recommendations for a more efficient organizational structure and administration and at the same time reviewing representation on the national executive committee. The document I prepared argued:

'The most efficient form of organization would be one united area facing each National Coal Board division, but excluding COSA, the Power Groups one and two and the Cokemens Area, in the case of Cokemen and COSA because they have separate conciliation schemes, and in the case of the groups because of agreements we have with the other unions concerned. This form of organizational structure would embrace all mineworkers employed under the terms and conditions negotiated under the provisions of the principal national conciliation scheme. In addition it would eliminate duplication and overlapping in the Unions' activities and administration and reduce the costs of such administration.'

In subsequent paragraphs, we showed that in each Coal Board division offices could be closed and administration could be concentrated at the most convenient centre. Suggestions were offered for changing the form of representation to the national executive committee to give craftsmen one-sixth of the places on the committee, that is, five out of a suggested thirty, with statutory conferences of craftsmens' representatives to consider their special occupational problems. The document set out in detail what effect the suggested changes would have on membership in the proposed consolidated areas and how an increase in specialist staff and services was possible without an increase in expenditure. No redundancy was involved, the suggestion being that staff adjustments should be spread over a period of time, cushioned by wastage and retirements.

The document was considered by the organizational subcommittee of the union at one of its infrequent meetings, and as I recall it now, attracted no support other than my own. So completely was it rejected that a decision was taken not to attach it to the minutes of the meeting, with the result that it was not even circulated to the rest of the executive committee!

It was clear that no kind of major reorganization was welcome and that the past practice of reviewing each situation when a union official retired would continue. Not until some time later was I told in confidence that the real reason for the rejection of the document was that the suggested reforms would have upset the balance between left and right in the union and would have strengthened the position of the left. I must admit that I had not given much thought to this possibility, but even if I had, on the principle of one union organization to face each division of the Coal Board, I could not have made changes that would alter this. In any event the effect on the relationship between left and right would still have maintained the right wing in a dominating position. The combination of this kind of political opposition and the vested interests of union officials who object to being disturbed from the thrones of their little empires was an obstruction too formidable to overcome, so that change in organizational structure proceeds slowly and in a piecemeal fashion. The miners' union could be a compact industrial union but it is still in effect a federation of areas, each holding on to a large measure of autonomy, with two, three or more constituent associations operating in single Coal Board areas and overlapping into others, each with its separate administrative offices, duplicating union services, all of which add substantially to the total administrative costs. Some day, perhaps, the membership will realize that by reorganizing union structure and administration, they could have their present service for a smaller union contribution, or, what is far preferable, a better service for the same contribution.

For about two-thirds of the time that I was an official of the miners' union, the coalmines were nationalized. On the whole, my relationships with the various leading personalities of the National Coal Board, at divisional and national level, have been good. This does not mean, of course, that there were no differences of opinion on policy matters; there were plenty and they were often fierce, but there was also a mutual respect for the man having the job to do. The first ten years were concentrated on short-term results to meet a coal famine, and the efforts of the engineers and technicians were geared to this aim. But during the second ten years the scene had changed and the emphasis had to be on increasing productivity and reducing production costs. This was the period when the drive in the industry to concentrate and rationalize production really got under way and was also the time of intense pre-occupation with the mechanization of all operations. The then chairman of the Board, Sir James Bowman, an ex-miner and ex-union official, had the big task of working this change of policy. The relationship between Jim Bowman and the union was a close one, more particularly perhaps, when Arthur Horner was in office. They had been close friends over a long period, and, through Horner, I too had known him for a very long time. To Bowman must go the credit for having laid the basis for the intensive mechanization of the industry and, in the first years of the slump in coal demand, for easing the effects upon pits and communities. When he retired in 1961, around thirty million tons of coal had been put to stock, otherwise far more pits would have closed from 1959 onwards. He was a chairman who trusted miners' leaders and who was able

150

to consult with them in an intimate way and take them into his confidence. This enabled the union on more than one occasion to anticipate events and be prepared to meet them.

His successor, Alfred Robens, was for most of us an unknown quantity, whose first speeches following the announcement of his appointment did not endear him to union leaders, for he said that he was not opposed to the plans for decentralization, whereas we were then strongly opposing them. However, we soon got to know him and to appreciate his qualities. To him must go the credit for projecting the image of the coal industry as a modernized forward-planning industry. He rapidly built on the basis laid by his predecessor and as he possessed a flair for publicity the changes being made in the industry were constantly before the public. There were times too, when the publicity for certain projects was exaggerated and over-dramatized, as in the case of the Beavercotes manless faces development, where the result claimed could not be realized. Nevertheless, his dynamic leadership forced big changes within the industry. He was, however, more of a powerful individual than the leader of a team of experts and specialists, as most of his predecessors had been. As I write this he has retired and his successor will not find it easy to replace him.

Naturally, I was sorry not to be able to continue working in the wider trade union movement but I was not at a loss for something to do. Being national secretary of the NUM was a full-time job, especially during the years of rapid contraction of the industry. I was deeply interested and involved in reforming the wages systems in the industry and in organizing discussions on the need to change the structure of the union and in promoting improved safety measures. Some success was achieved in 1966 by the introduction of the National Power Loading Agreement, but changing union structure was painfully slow to get moving, although the registration provisions of the new Industrial Relations Bill may now stimulate greater interest and speed. The final achievement, realized as my retirement arrived, was the launching of the union's own monthly journal, *The Miner*, a need accelerated by the Coal Board's house publication *Coal News*.

Here was the employer communicating direct with his employees, mostly members of the union. Often his communications were ahead of those of the union, and sometimes contrary to union policy. During the paper's first years, many complaints were received from lodges and areas, not only against its content, but against the methods adopted to secure its wide distribution. But like most other innovations there follows a process of adaptation and adjustment on both sides that leads to toleration, if not acceptance. The Board's monthly production undoubtedly accelerated the union's resolution requesting the executive committee to 'investigate the need for developing a national journal' which was debated and carried at the union's annual conference in 1962. The first issue, however, was not published until January 1969 – after an interval of more than six years. The fact is that there was a strong silent opposition to its production and this opposition was political in character. There were, in the interval, many meetings, much research into costing and methods of distribution. All the obstacles raised were investigated and ways proposed for overcoming them, but the enthusiasm for the project was lacking. There was concern that the paper might become a medium for purveying left-wing views, and give publicity to the views of those contesting for leadership in the union.

I think these were very real and genuine concerns for some of the executive committee and for whom such considerations would outweigh any advantages such a journal would have for the union as a whole. The problems had to be argued fully, and it is probably pretty near the truth to state that the paper was launched despite the executive committee. I agree that the paper should not be just a vehicle for left-wing views, but should be open to all views, right, left or centre, with the policy statements based on conference or executive committee decisions. It is important for a paper of this kind to open its pages to the rank and file and to encourage discussion of all points of view. It must become a union paper in every sense, otherwise it is bound to fail. Anyway, *The Miner* is now launched, being produced monthly, with a subeditor who was appointed before I retired. I think I can claim the major responsibility for finally getting it started, although the first publication did not come until the month after I had left. The first issue had a middle-page spread devoted to a tribute to me, written by John Cole, news editor of The *Guardian*. In the second issue, the back page carried a headline, based on a news item from South Wales, 'Paynter Condemned by Welsh Miners'. Such is the uncertainty of trade union popularity! The condemnation concerned my acceptance of an appointment to the Commission on Industrial Relations, and it was made by the executive committee of the South Wales area of the union.

Chapter 10

Retirement and New Responsibilities

I must frankly confess that I did not look forward to retirement with any relish. I was afraid of the effect of both physical and mental idleness. I gave some consideration to a post I had been offered before my actual retirement early in December, as a part-time member of a nationalized industry, but could not accept it, for to do so would have been to repudiate policies with which I had been identified for most of my life. During the months before my retirement I had been invited to functions organized to mark my retirement in pretty well all areas of the coalfield. In all of them, particularly the huge gathering in South Wales, speakers said that it would be a great shame and scandal if my services and talents were not used. The general feeling was that I should be given a responsible job where my experience and ability could be put to good use. This, too, was the view quite a few industrial writers expressed in their columns. Who but the Government were likely to find some continued use for me? However, having turned down their offer of a part-time post, I considered it extremely unlikely that any further offers would be made, and so I occupied myself in writing a book dealing with problems of trade unionism. By the end of February 1969, I had completed the first draft and sent it for critical examination by a journalist friend. There was some delay, however, and the book was not published until the spring of 1970.

At this point I should explain that when I retired from my job in the union I also retired from the Communist Party. In fact I informed the Edgware branch dues collector of my decision early in December, long before I was approached to take a full-time job. This was not a sudden decision but was in accordance with a family understanding decided on many years before. There is, I suppose, an advantage in having a relatively unusual name during ballots or elections because it is easily remembered, but when one is on the receiving end of public hostility, as I was from time to time, this can be a handicap and was the cause of some unpleasantness not only for me but for members of my family. I was very often the subject of attack from newspapers, the medium through which so many people derive their opinions. The worst experience came during the Hungarian uprising, when it became risky for me to go into my local pub where I had been going for years because this hostility against me threatened to become violent. I was fortunate in having some good hefty friends. But the position became extremely difficult for my older sons who were then attending grammar school. I did not know of it until later, but they had a bad time until their headmaster got to hear of it and intervened to stop it. Feelings against me and my family had been incited by an open letter published in the South Wales edition of the *Empire News*, a Sunday paper being published in Cardiff during 1956. The letter, written by Mr David Llewellyn, then Member of Parliament for Cardiff North, associated me as a communist with the bloodshed in Budapest, the murder of little children and the other terrible things that were happening there. In the family discussions about this situation I had to make my position clear. It was not possible for me to leave the Communist Party just because such intimidation was being directed against me; it would be cowardly and unprincipled to leave in such circumstances. At the time, however, it would have been easy to take such a decision and I almost did at one point during this harrowing experience, but found that I just could not. Attempts to force me to take a decision provoke the opposite reaction in me. Nor could I take such a step either then or now, knowing that it would be used to support unprincipled attacks on the Communist Party. I despise ex-communists who lend themselves to such attacks. I left the party quietly and it was first given publicity by the Party itself when they criticized me for accepting an appointment to the Commission on Industrial Relations. As far as I know, the government did not know either; I certainly did not inform them and felt under no obligation to do so.

The proposal for a Commission on Industrial Relations came from the report of the Donovan Commission; from the start I saw it as a useful and constructive piece of machinery and said so. I have thought for a long time that, in the interests of trade union and working class unity, some basic reforms on a voluntary basis should be encouraged and that an organization should be set up to do this. I believe that the reform of industrial relations requires that far fewer unions should operate in the same plant or company; that wages systems need to be modernized and made relevant to the new production techniques; and that bargaining procedures need to be far more explicit. The Commission on Industrial Relations, working on a purely voluntary basis, seemed ideal for the job. I do not see it as anti-trade union or as a restriction of the freedom to strike. Its powers were restricted to presenting the facts after an examination in depth and its recommendations operated only if they were voluntarily accepted by all the parties to a dispute. Had the Commission been set up independently of the other proposals outlined in the Labour government's White Paper *In Place of Strife*, there could have been little opposition to it. As it happened, however, it was included in the White Paper and, in the agitation against sanctions, the good and bad proposals were lumped together, as part of a package deal to be wholly rejected. This was, it appeared, the line taken by the militant movement, but the official line of the TUC supported the proposals it considered constructive and opposed the parts it considered objectionable. It supported the setting up of the Commission, and, with the exception of the Draughtsmen's Association, the trade union movement has co-operated in the work of the Commission at national, district and plant level. Once the White Paper was withdrawn, opposition to the Commission ceased, even from those shop stewards who had previously supported the militant line.

In Place of Strife was provocative and stupid. Like the Industrial Relations Act of the Tory government, it sees unofficial strikes as the target – and not the situation that causes them. My whole experience of investigating industrial relations procedures

156

and institutions with the CIR confirms that the cause of most unofficial strikes can be found in the wages systems, and those cannot be changed by legislation. They can only be changed by voluntary agreement. However, the Tory policy has far more fundamental political aims. Unofficial strikes are to be curbed but, more important, official trade union action is to be restricted, and the unions put into a legal strait-jacket. The purpose is twofold – to counter the stronger bargaining position of the unions under conditions of full employment, and by this means to effect some restraint and control over the size of wage increases.

The incidence of unofficial strikes should not be the main worry either of governments or the trade union movement, and it is pretty futile to defend them by arguing that more days are lost by strikes in some other country, or that the effect of accidents and sickness exerts a far more disastrous effect on productivity. Such arguments may be true and justified, but they are directed to the incidence of such strikes, whereas the real menace to society is in their character. They are mainly sectional strikes invariably confined to a particular occupational group, who in the chain system of production can put thousands out of work, not only in a particular plant, but in plants scattered all over the country. It is not the effect that such strikes have upon production that worries me, but the way they affect the social outlook of the people. Such strikes encourage the philosophy that individual and sectional interests transcend those of the mass; individualism and sectionalism are enhanced as a strategy, as a concept for social progress, and as the basis of a new philosophy in the trade union movement. I have spent a lifetime in the trade union movement as a revolutionary socialist, and this strategy and philosophy is opposed to everything that I was taught and to everything I believe as being necessary to the advance of socialism. If there is one lesson to be drawn from the history of the working class, or from the small facet of it presented in this narrative, it is that unity is paramount. The maxim on so many trade union banners – 'United we stand, divided we fall' – is the philosophy of a century of struggle and sacrifice, of the 'blood, tears, toil and sweat' of a host of trade union and socialist pioneers.

It is my view that the recommendations of the Donovan Com-

157

mission have been interpreted in a way that encourages this sectional development. Donovan concluded that the formal institutions had lost control, that is, the trade unions and employers' associations, and that their wage bargaining was no longer realistic. The real bargaining was plant bargaining, and it was recommended that this should be formalized. The interpretation in practice has tended to consolidate this form of bargaining and even to extend it, to the detriment of company-wide and industry-wide wage bargaining. Surely the more the wage bargaining system is fragmented, the more numerous the disparities and differentials and the more dominant is the individual and sectional approach to wage problems. I can understand the support and promotion of this development by those who believe that the way forward to end capitalism and achieve socialism is to create as much dislocation, disorder and anarchy as possible in the belief that this will bring about the collapse of capitalism, and that out of the chaos socialist organization and leadership will emerge. It is my belief that organization and leadership has to be built before and during the struggle against capitalism, and that it is in this process that socialist consciousness is created among the mass of the people. It is the working class aspect of the struggle that has to be emphasized; that is where the unity has to be forged. It seems to me that individual and sectional action can militate against the long-term interests of working people, and that it is a concept giving short-term gains only to the strongest, with the weakest going to the wall, and whose adoption by working people offers a free-for-all private enterprise philosophy of capitalism, in opposition to the organization and collectivism of socialism.

As I have stated earlier, my work with the CIR tends to confirm these strongly held views. I recall in the early months that, when the battle against the White Paper held up our terms of reference, I was asked to lead an investigation into containerization and its consequences on the transport industries. We had to suspend the investigation when references were made, but not before we had gathered a good deal of information. We visited several docks, and met both dock employers and union leaders. It was obvious that the wages systems in operation were out of date, and

158

this too, was the conclusion of the Devlin Commission. In Liverpool, there were so many elements in the make-up of wages, relating to occupation, commodities, piece-work, and 'impedences', that it is really surprising that there were not more strikes there. I was requested by the dock employers to attend a seminar they organized to discuss the changes in wages systems made in other industries. It was not possible for me to do so other than explain the changes we had made in the mining industry. Any changes in the wages system in dockland must evolve from their own conditions. In fact, discussions were proceeding on the second stage of the Devlin recommendations which involved a complete overhaul of the wages set-up and this has now been concluded.

We found the same evidence of out-dated systems in most of the other company or industry references we investigated, as the published reports show. Generally, they revealed a wages build-up from a large number of separate items and the more the items the more were the points at which dispute could arise. It was not the Commission's job to suggest how such systems should be changed but to report that some change was necessary, and it was for the parties in the established bargaining procedures to agree and effect the changes. But frequently, too, the bargaining procedures were inadequate and very often fragmented. In some undertakings, each union insisted on its own separate negotiating machinery, where joint negotiations were absent or extremely weak. This of course is the by-product of a situation where several unions operate in the same plant and department. We could recommend 'one union, one plant' but invariably the outcome was more likely to be a compromise, and if agreement could be obtained on 'spheres of influence' between competing unions, it represented some progress. The difficulties of the Commission were greatest in references involving claims by unions for recognition in plants or companies where this was refused by the employers. Employers' resistance was strongest when such claims involved white-collar workers. In a few of these references, although the recommendation was for either full or partial recognition, employers refused to accept the recommendation, and one was forced to consider the question of whether legal compulsion should be applied. For the Commission to operate on a mixture of voluntarism and compulsion would, in my view, have eroded the goodwill of employers and unions without which it could not function effectively. Such a body must be completely removed from legal enforcement if it is to be useful in promoting industrial relations reform.

My acceptance of the appointment was condemned partly because the Commission was seen as a government agent, but as it has functioned under Royal Warrant, it was not a government agency. No predetermined criteria were laid down as in the case of the Prices and Incomes Board; there was no consultation with the government in the preparation of reports and recommendations or in the determination of the methods by which the Commission operated; it functioned independently of any government department. Of course, references were routed through a government department, and the Commission came into being as a result of a government decision, but the government in no way influenced the methods by which such references should be dealt with, and indeed the Commission could also influence the kind of references routed to it. The Commission was as independent as any body set up by a government could be. It had nothing to do with strikes or wage levels; it was not a conciliatory agency for settling disputes; its function was long-term – to investigate in depth and to recommend and get agreement, by persuasion only, on reforms in the institutions and procedures of industrial relations. It is because I saw it as this kind of institution that I accepted an appointment to it, and became more convinced from the experience of working in it that it could make a useful contribution in promoting voluntary reform. The final reference I was involved in, which we concluded on the last day I was with the CIR, had started months earlier in face of opposition from some district officials of important trade unions. During the investigation there was more than one strike, one or two of them prolonged, but we still had consultations with the shop stewards on the general situation, although obviously not on the issues of the strike. We had many meetings with the senior stewards and union officials, and two meetings with them and the employers' representatives together. In the end, at their request, we drafted the collective bargaining agreement and the grievance procedure for the plants operating for the company. We discussed the drafts and amended them following such discussions, and in the final get-together of employers, union officers and senior stewards we were not only thanked for the work we had done but were made a presentation by one of the union officers who initially had opposed our investigation – a presentation not just to me, but to the whole team who had undertaken the investigation and who had established warm and friendly relations with both the stewards and union officers.

When the full implication of the Conservative government's intentions in the proposed new legislation was revealed in the consultative document, I reached a decision as to my own future with the Commission. I could not accept, in the first place, that any significant improvement in industrial relations could be achieved by measures of legal compulsion. Such measures are more likely to incite than to appease, and in any event were likely to be changed again when the next Labour government was elected to power. Industrial relations and trade union and employer relations are not likely to be assisted by this kind of political knock-about. In the second place, it reminded me of 1927, when a previous Conservative government introduced legislation to contain trade disputes and trade unions. I had fought against it then and could hardly approve of even stricter legal measures now. Putting trade unions in a tighter legal strait-jacket is a basic element in Tory philosophy, and not just an expedient to meet a particular situation. The position in 1927 was entirely different to that in 1971. Then, the unions were extremely weak, with non-unionism at its height and company unions operating in important industries. Then, there was mass unemployment with the supply of labour outstripping demand by millions. In 1927, the employers were in the ascendant having defeated the General Strike. The reason then for the legislation against trade unions was not that they were too strong or that unofficial strikes were proliferating the scene, but to take advantage of the weakness of unions to shackle them, and thus to secure a permanent advantage for the employers in industrial bargaining. The reason today still accords with this basic thinking. In this setting of relatively full employment, the bargaining

L

advantage is with the unions and workers and the real aim of the legislation is to adjust this relationship to the advantage of the employer. Free play of market forces in determining trade relations between firms and countries is glorified but not in the labour market. Here the price of labour is not to be determined by the free play of market forces but is to be held in check – not by a legislated policy of wage restraint but by strengthening the bargaining position of the employers in relation to the unions. The power of the unions and workers in exploiting the favourable market position is curtailed by restricting union activity and imposing penal reprisals against unofficial strikers and their leaders. The main emphasis of the legal enforcement will be directed against the shop stewards, the union representatives in industry responsible for wage negotiations.

These being my general views of the proposed legislation, I decided to resign from the Commission. On 21 October, I addressed a letter to the Secretary of State for Employment briefly setting out my views and intimating my intention to resign. At that time the Commission was considering removing itself a stage further away from the Industrial Court to make it more acceptable to the trade unions. I did not agree, and in the letter to the Minister I made it clear that 'no change in detail affecting the functioning of the CIR will alter the fact that the CIR will be an integral part of a comprehensive plan which will have the effect of restricting the freedom of the trade unions'. I reminded the Minister that when I accepted appointment it was to 'promote voluntary reform of institutions and procedures of collective bargaining in a legal background free from any threat of legal enforcement of recommended reforms'. The government's proposals radically altered the conditions which applied when the post was offered and accepted and it was no longer possible for me to 'serve in a body intended to form part of such a legal framework and in face of the united opposition of the trade union and Labour movement'.

I received a very courteous letter from the secretary of State, as could be expected, expressing regret at my decision and appreciation for the service I had given. In my letter to him, I acknowledged the difficulties that might be created by my immediate retirement and which were due to the illness of a Commission colleague and to the fact that I was in the final stages of completing a particular reference, where it would have been difficult for someone else to take over the final discussions. However, I wrote again that my resignation would become effective from 30 November, and so by the second anniversary of my retirement from the Miners' Union I had been in and out of a job, highly paid for a man like me. I have no regrets either for accepting the appointment or for resigning from it when circumstances changed. It was very interesting work and sometimes exciting in its encounters. It certainly increased my understanding of the problems of other industries and unions, and my knowledge of the pretty hopeless mess of the institutions and procedures of collective bargaining in some important industries. A big job needs to be done in this field but I think that it can only be done by a body operating on an entirely voluntary basis.

It was hinted when I accepted the appointment to the Commission that I had done so for the money involved. The annual salary of £6,500 was apparently my price for desertion, the thirty pieces of silver for betrayal. In fact I received one letter which quoted in full Browning's *Lost Leader* which starts: 'Just for a handful of silver he left us, Just for a ribbon to pin on his breast.' There were far more letters, however, supporting my acceptance, many of them from long-standing friends in the Communist Party. The salary was not a decisive factor – either when I accepted the job or when I decided to withdraw from it. I have been criticized in the Communist Party for lacking ambition and I have a history of resisting plans aimed at pushing me into higher posts in the union. In any case, my need for money at sixtyfive years old was far less than it was at fortyfive, when I had five children under five years of age.

Looking back I cannot find anything in my past activities which suggests that I was ever particularly concerned with money rewards, and there was a time when I could have earned more as a miner than I could as a union officer. What people say about a particular individual is not very important but what does matter is the belief that any working class leader who accepts a post with a relatively high salary (and these days £6,500 cannot be considered very high) has deserted the cause with which he has hitherto been identified. There are, today, plenty of trade union leaders and Labour politicians whose incomes far exceed the salaries paid at the CIR – as often as not for less constructive service. The test, it seems to me, must be based on the nature of the job accepted and the use the individual tries to make of it, and whether there is evidence of a change in outlook and policy. In these days, when greater participation by workers and trade unionists in the management of industry is demanded, at some stage such people must accept appointments to management posts at higher salaries. To feel the need to pass judgment on whether or not a person has deserted his class origin and interests is a good healthy sign but it must be based on something more tangible than monetary rewards if the judgment is to be fair and just. The criticism directed against me soon abated and had no permanent effect upon the long-standing friendship even of those who criticized me. I make no apology for what happened and still consider that I was right to accept the appointment – and right to terminate it when I did.

Chapter 11

Conclusion

In the foregoing pages I have attempted to give some account of the activities of the 'angry young men' of my generation. The account is limited by my own limitations as a narrator, and by the boundaries of my own experience and activities. The account is effectively in two parts, the one in the interwar years, when my generation was fighting defensive battles against wage attacks, unemployment, fascism and war, and the other in the post-war period, when in relatively full employment the battle has been an offensive one, for higher standards of living, for greater freedom and participation in the affairs of the nation, for peace between nations, and the banning of the most diabolical of all war weapons, the hydrogen bomb. The first part of the story told of the lockouts, the strikes against wage cuts, the spasmodic attempts at unified resistance of trade unions, through first, the Triple Alliance, and second, the General Strike. This is followed by an account of the violent years of struggle against unemployment, of mass poverty and privation, accompanied by vicious police repression. Interwoven into the account is the story of the continuous resistance to fascism both in this country, in Spain and in Germany, which finally culminated in a second world war. There were many weaknesses and deficiencies in our struggles, but it is a record of which my generation is entitled to be proud and which merits the commendation of the generations that follow. When a comprehensive history of the period is written it will rate high in relation to any other epic period of working class history.

In the post-war years, our role in history-making changed to a concentration on raising living standards. Although the account in this narrative is mainly concerned with the mining industry, the scene of my own activities, it is typical of the change being

165

effected in the conditions of all industrial and service workers in the country, the changes resulting in the creation of what is called the Welface State, in the extension of nationalization, in the maintenance of full employment, and not least in transforming the role and status of the trade union movement in the affairs of the state. There have been many reverses too, but the overall result, unlike the position in the interwar years, which was characterized by successive defeats, is a post-war progressive general improvement in the important aspects of life. This is the effective contrast, but it does not mean that everything necessary has been done. It is a record, however, of considerable progress on the important fronts of human activity.

There is a tendency for the younger modern generation to deride and degenerate the older one as stick-in-the-mud and reactionary. This I see as the natural and age-old relationship of youth and age, referred to in the opening pages of this story. The youth of today will be the elders of tomorrow and they too will be denigrated by their successors. What is important is that the achievements and difficulties of earlier generations should be understood and appreciated. This is the case, generally speaking, in the assessment of the more distant past, but is rarely so in the case of the immediate past. It is hoped that some young people who may read these pages will be helped to understand and appreciate the efforts of my generation.

My concern in the past and for the future is with the promotion of the labour and trade union movement towards socialism. The economic and political environment has undergone significant changes within which progress to this goal has to be made both now and in the future. Alongside public ownership in Britain is the development towards ever greater economic organization, both national and international, in the private sector. The great industrial and commercial enterprises of modern society spread their activities in many countries and are international in character. There has been a strengthening of the role of money, made necessary by the huge capital requirements of the new technological age, with the result that the financial structures of the industrial nations are interdependent and closely integrated. The money world is dominated by international capital and banks.

This country seems hell bent on joining the Common Market, a development which will significantly change the economic and political environment for the advance of socialism. Add to this the constant danger of local wars mounting into global wars, and the international character of the present and future situation is apparent. To this add the problems of racial integration, the position of Jews in the world, the potential of nuclear and germ warfare in the relationships of nations, and the emphasis for forward strategy seems clearly an international concern. This, in my view, is a central consideration for the modern labour and trade union movement.

The need for international trade union unity, seen against this background, is urgent both for economic and political reasons. That a common front must be established against international companies is already accepted by some of the more progressive unions, but it is usually limited to consultations with American or certain European unions. Far wider consultation is needed to pave the way for organizational unity. The economic problems, important though they are, are overshadowed by the political, which are concerned with issues of human survival. There should be closer consultation between the unions in capitalist countries with those in socialist countries. Put shortly, world international trade union unity needs to be re-established.

I recall moving a resolution in a Miners' Annual Conference in 1949, just after the splitting-up of the world Federation of Trade Unions, which called upon the National Executive Committee to 'use its influence to heal the breach which now exists between the British Trade Unions and the WFTU'. The arguments I used then to justify steps to restore unity apply with, if anything more force now :

> 'After all, the World Federation of Trade Unions was born out of the unity of the workers in the capitalist world and the workers of the socialist world; they united in common against a common enemy – fascism.'

The only change needed in that sentence to make it relevant today, would be to substitute 'war' for 'fascism'. International trade union unity then came about as a result of the initiative

167

taken by the British TUC through the Anglo-Russian Trade Union Committee. The only opposition to world unity came from the American Federation of Labour, and it is likely that they would still oppose it, judging by George Meany's attitude in the International Federation of Trade Unions over the past few years. His anti-communism is extreme and will probably influence the attitude of the American unions while he still retains control, but this is no obstacle to the British TUC taking the intiative in opening discussions, as they did in 1945.

War is greatly feared both by the leaders and the people of the socialist countries. I have led many delegations of miners to these countries, and acted as host to many of their delegations to Britain. As far back as 1953, we had a delegation of Chinese miners in South Wales and sent one to China. I have been on such visits to the Soviet Union on three occasions, to Czechoslovakia twice, to Poland and Hungary, and if there is one subject we are always pressed to discuss, either in their countries or here, it is peace. The miners have been constant in maintaining friendly relations with these countries through such exchanges of delegations, and have been constant, too, in their support for international trade unity when the matter has been discussed in Congress.

To justify their break with the international trade unions in 1948, the British trade union leaders declared that the communist unions used it as a medium for spreading communist propaganda, but the break actually took place following Churchill's 1946 'cold war' speech in America, and the innovation of Marshall Aid in the western world, to which there were very clearly political strings, as witness the repudiation by British leaders of the French miners' strike. But whatever the reasons, and there was probably fault on both sides, it is not a sound argument against restoring world trade union unity in the 1970s. If world peace is to be preserved and the centres of tension eased, I believe that the workers in all lands have together to exert pressure upon governments, for when they are organized and united they represent a power far greater than that of any government.

High on my list of priorities for future political strategy I would note the need for the leaders of this dynamic modern gene-

168

ration to work for the unity of the progressive political organizations in Britain. Her internal problems are too serious to be tackled by a fragmented working class movement, involving as they do such issues as the prices and income policy, trade union legislation, whether by resistance to it or to its ultimate repeal, the Common Market, defence policy, racial policy, and economic and social growth. Differing attitudes towards these issues exist both within Britain and within the international movement, but they have to be assessed against the paramount needs of people. Sincerity is not a quality exclusive to a particular political party and the political judgment of all parties and their leaders can be wrong. Bigotry wherever it exists is a powerful opponent of progress and an equally powerful cause of strife and disunity. The 'holier than thou' attitude has bedevilled the working class political scene for too long, and whether one is a communist or a social democrat, common ground can be found for unity, especially unity in action even if limited in form, as in 1935 and 1936 against the means test. A little less political snobbery everywhere would help in this.

Unity is still the theme, in this instance for trade union organization within industry. When my previous book was reviewed, some critics suggested that a more unified trade union structure would be realized only when a socialist Britain was created and that to contend for it now was to create a diversion from the struggle against capitalism. As stated earlier, leaders can make errors of political judgment and this can certainly apply to me, but in my political judgment, such as it is, I believe that unity in all forms of working class organization is a necessary precondition for a socialist Britain. I have visited plants and factories where as many as fifteen separate unions have operated in the same production department, not always in cooperation, and where the service from hard-worked union officers was restricted by the numerous plants and industries their duties covered. Even where union administration was organized on an industrial basis, the area covered could be so large and scattered that leadership tended to be remote from the members at factory level. Or sometimes branch organization was divorced from industry and from the problems of members at their place of work, and very often

169

the shop steward had no formal obligation to the branch. This state of affairs is not an indication of trade union strength and does not in my opinion represent effective trade union organization in industry. For union organization to be effective, it must be based on a particular industry and not, as it is now, spread over a large number of them. Such a change obviously requires planning and could only be effected progressively over a period of time, but a start has to be made sometime. A trade union structure related to the structure of industry, vertical and not horizontal, will certainly be necessary to the general structure of a socialist society, but I consider it equally necessary as the most effective form of trade union organization even in a capitalist society. In addition, the role of the TUC in modern conditions is vastly changed, but its organization and authority have not advanced with these changes and there is need for far stronger central leadership. The Trades Union Congress, representing the affiliated unions, is now involved daily in politics. Hardly a reform in industry can be made now that does not involve the central government. In fact, industry and government are now so closely interrelated that every important industrial question is a political issue including, as is readily apparent, wages. This involvement when a Conservative government is in power, can in my view sometimes make the trade union movement a far more effective political opposition than the Parliamentary Labour Party. The TUC pronouncements on economic and financial policy and their proposals for national policy each year indicate that they now project alternative government policies in this field. Their political opposition to the Industrial Relations Bill is far more powerful than any opposition from within Parliament could be. This new position arises from the changing character of relationships within modern society. They could, I suspect, considerably influence the future relations between the trade union movement and the Parliamentary Labour Party. Trade union dependence upon a political party in the House of Commons to represent their views has gone; the trade union movement itself now puts its own point of view direct and governments consult it on all matters of major policy. This is why I consider the restructuring and centralizing of power of the trade unions to be such an important project for the future.

170

One thing I am certain of as far as the future is concerned is that modern youth will not tolerate the poverty and repression that my generation did in its youth; that it will not do so is because our struggle for improvement has brought great changes. Poverty was the common lot of working people – the condition into which we were born. There is poverty now, it is true, but it is not as widespread nor, where it exists, as severe as it was in my child-hood. Our expectations from life were less than the expections of the modern generation, and poverty today has to be measured against this and should be compared not with the past but with the possibilities for a better life that the present can offer. What were inaccessible luxuries for us are in many instances now ac-cepted as everyday necessities. This is the new starting point for progress today. This is the foundation that my generation helped to lay and upon which future progress can be built.

To bring this personal epistle to an end, I should like to quote the last sentences of a Presidential Address I made to a South Wales Miners' Conference in 1958 which seems an appropriate message today.

'We are living in a world of contradictions and contrasts. On the one side, miracles of scientific achievement; the discovery of new sources of energy and heat open before us new vistas of limitless progress and development toward human security and happiness, a million times more revolutionary than the discovery of fire was for primitive society.

'The release of human labour by automatic mechanical pro-cesses could offer men, with the prospect of more leisure, the opportunity to pursue higher forms of culture with the concept of a better life. But, although man can now scale the highest peaks and the poles of the earth and can travel into outer space, we are living in a period when either a new species of man will evolve or where man and life on earth will be com-pletely destroyed because, on the other side of the picture, instead of increased security and happiness, we face increased redundancy and the spectre of unemployment; cuts in real wages and social services and of increased rents. In short, we face the prospect of greater poverty, instead of increased leisure

171

for those who toil, the prospect of harder work and more exploitation. The conquest of nature, instead of creating greater freedom for man, enforces new enslavement where personal freedom for individuals and families is walled in by a secret terror masquerading as 'security'. Instead of offering a future of limitless progress, the new discoveries of heat and energy threaten civilization with universal disease and death. In a word, the miracles of scientific achievements made possible by man's genius instead of being used to uplift mankind as a whole, are exploited to increase the wealth, privilege and power of a few. We have reached a point in the history of society when we have to choose either to live on in a new society or to die with the old.

'The new discoveries cannot be used to the advantage of mankind in a society where production, distribution and exchange is a jungle of competing interests for private profit. The great changes in production techniques based on a new source of power in a capitalist economy threaten the working people with unemployment and misery. These great discoveries can only be applied and developed to the advantage of all in a socialist society, where there is no exploitation of labour and no production for profit. Private ownership of the means of production must be replaced by social ownership which will remove the barriers to sane economic planning and which alone can ensure that the new processes will be used to the benefit of the people as a whole.

'A socialist Britain is no longer an ideal for the distant future. It is imperative now, and can be realized now by the will and power of the organized Labour and Trade Union movement. Let us all unite our forces in these days so fraught with peril to the peace of the world, so menacing to the security and happiness of our people.'

My views are the same now as they were then and I do not regret the path that these views led me to follow. With the poet, I can say :

> 'Yet would I tread again, all the road over,
> Face the old joy and pain, hemlock and clover.'